D1256908

The Promise

By the same author:

KIERKEGAARD AND RADICAL DISCIPLESHIP
HIS END UP: GETTING GOD INTO THE NEW THEOLOGY

The Promise:

Ethics in the Kingdom of God

————◄◆►————

VERNARD ELLER

DOUBLEDAY & COMPANY, INC., GARDEN CITY, NEW YORK
1970

To
THE CHRISTIAN CENTURY
a pretty premise
even if the magazine contributes more
to books like this
than it does to centenary celestialism

Table of Contents

The Why and Wherefore to Be Never Minded

Once upon a time (though it wasn't really all that long ago) *The Christian Century* published an article which struck me as being of considerable significance. The fact that it was *my* article might have had something to do with this reaction.

But more to the point, Doubleday & Company (or if not Doubleday, at least a member of the company) read it and shared my impression to the extent of inviting me to do a book on the subject—which is what you now hold.

The only place to start is at the beginning, with the original article. It follows; and what follows it is that which since has been prodded loose by Doubleday—just one demanded thing after another.

The Promise

1

The
Ethic of Promise

———◆———

If the theology of promise (or what some people may still insist on calling "the theology of hope") ever is to make anything of itself, sooner or later it will need to develop a department of ethics. What follows are some preliminary thoughts in that direction.

Contextualist

An ethic of promise will be *contextualist*—but it will build upon a radically changed understanding of what constitutes a decision's context. In current ethical thought (whether or not this is the deepest intention of the theorists) contextualism has to do with discovering what action will be most beneficial for the persons directly involved in the immediate situation. Although not denying the validity of this consideration, advocates of the theology of promise would maintain that it is too narrow a perspective, both as to temporal scope and as to breadth of application.

The controlling factor of any situation, they would say, is not simply what its here-and-now implications are but how it relates to the overarching purpose and goal of history, which is the coming kingdom of God. Therefore, not "What will be the effect of this action in the immediacy of the moment or upon the immediate future of the participants?" but "How will this action gear in with God's ultimate in-

tention for mankind and the world?" Therefore, not "What
will this action do to the personal development of you and
me?" but "What does our action say about the growth of
humanity toward the kingdom of God?" These are the
proper formulations of the contextual question.

Obviously, the two sets of questions are not totally dis-
similar; in many cases they undoubtedly would lead to the
same choice. However, it is quite conceivable that situations
would arise in which the participants might choose to sacrifice their own welfare for the sake of the larger, longer-
range goal. In any case, those who hold to the theology of
promise would insist that the context of present actions
must be seen as including much more than simply the present. The truest thing that can be said about the present
is that it is God's future in process of becoming—and ethical decisions must be oriented toward that future.

Absolutist

An ethic of promise will be *absolutist*—but it will involve
a radically changed understanding of what constitutes the
absolute. Though the adjectives "contextualist" and "absolutist" are not usually applied to the same ethic, they can
be. However, as regards the theology of promise, the absolute is not a code that *has been* decreed in the past but a
promise of what *shall be* in the future. And that makes a
whale of a lot of difference!

Yet "absolute" is the only term that properly describes
the focus of eschatological theology, even if this is a reality
which does not yet exist. The outcome of history is fixed
absolutely—fixed by the promise and commitment, by the
past and present actions of God. And God is lord in such
sense that his promise of what "shall be" carries a stronger
guarantee than does the scientist's description of what "is
right now." This "kingdom that shall be" also is absolute
in the sense that nothing greater can be conceived beyond
it, that it will be total and universal in its scope. And if

we may say so, the absolute kingdom of God is something much more real, existential, concrete, and well defined than that so very elusive absolute: the abstract, make-of-it-what-you-will principle, LUV. It has come to pass in our day (that Scripture might be fulfilled): "Love" covers a multitude of sins—though somehow I can't quite think that that is what Scripture had in mind.

But an absolutist ethic that centers on an absolute *future* in many respects will be the direct contrary of one that takes its absolute from the *past*. An absolutist past necessarily takes the form of a record, a prescription, a decree. These items inevitably fall under the control of man, because the past is precisely that area of his experience in which man can select, interpret, and manipulate. And thus an absolutist decree is wide open for the misuses of legalism, moralism, and authoritarianism—some men dictating to and pushing around other men.

When, on the other hand, the absolute lies in the future it is in a province of God that man cannot tamper with. The absolute no longer is a prescription that tells man what he *has* to be; it is a description of (and a challenge to) what he *can* be and *shall* be. Here, then, is an absolutism that preserves the stability and sense of direction which the new morality has lost and yet divests itself of the inhumane legalism against which the new morality rightfully revolted.

Perfectionist

An ethic of promise will be *perfectionist*—but it will be tempered by a radically changed understanding of what "perfectionism" means.

Because its norm is "the present situation" (which of course always falls far short of perfection), the new morality shows up as anything but perfectionist. For that reason it too often becomes an excuse to settle for actions that are much less than the best. But the kingdom of God, which is the norm of the ethic of promise, can be called "perfection" in the fullest sense of that term.

However, the ethic of promise will differ from earlier forms of perfectionism in that its adherents will make no claim of having attained, or of being able immediately to attain, perfection. Whatever the ethical accomplishments achieved, it will be confessed that, compared to their goal, they are only feeble efforts, that they represent but paltry progress—but, even so, the efforts made are real, and real progress is made toward the perfect Not Yet which nevertheless shall be.

This perfectionism of the Not Yet will, of course, cut the ground from under customary types of perfectionist pride and self-righteousness. Yet it will provide some incentive that the new morality does not. Certainly God cannot help one achieve more than he is willing to attempt. And the new thrust of Jesus' promise, "You shall be [you actually *shall be*] perfect as your Father in heaven is perfect, [Concordant Literal translation]" opens the way for God to give true ethical greatness. For it tells man that he doesn't have to settle for anything less than perfection (which is to say that he had better not "settle" *yet*).

Heroic

Whatever else may be said for the new morality, it hardly can be described as an ethic that inspires heroism. Although again contrary to what its founders must have purposed, it tends to become quite self-serving—almost a method for doing what you want without having to feel guilty about it afterward. Very seldom does it speak in terms of self-denial and sacrifice.

The ethic of promise, on the other hand, is of a different stripe. It breaks through the narrow horizon of little old "me and thee (and sometimes I wonder about thee)" to focus upon God's grand design and destiny for the race. And within that setting men can be challenged to acts of

ethical daring, can be made willing to expend themselves
and their private interests for the sake of humanity's move
toward the kingdom.

Tension-Producing

On first thought, this feature of the ethic of promise may
seem to be a handicap; it is, however, a real strength.

Again, whether or not it was in the intention of its first
proponents, the new morality has had the rather clear effect
of accommodating Christian ethical teaching to the accepted
level of society at large. This, of course, serves to relax
the tension between Christianity and the world, to make
them quite comfortable with each other.

Not so with the ethic of promise. The fact that it operates
out of a different context, that it marches to the beat of a
different drummer (the future kingdom of God rather than
the present kingdom of this world), is bound to put it into
rather severe tension with the world. To have one segment
of society, the Christian minority, pushing ahead toward
its absolutist, perfectionist goal will not set too well with
the majority whose only interest is to accommodate to the
world as it is. Indeed, in some situations this "ethic that
refuses to wait" could pose an actual threat to what society
understands as its self-interest—if, for example, those who
accept the promise of the peaceable kingdom were to decide that they no longer *have* to let themselves be sucked
into the world's violent ways.

This ethic would produce not simply tension but trauma.
Yet, bear in mind that it was the very Lord of the Promise
who said, "I have not come to bring peace, but a sword."
There is a trauma of birth as well as of death; the ethic of
promise can be expected to bring on the birth pangs of
the kingdom. Its proponents will make no claim that its
methods will "work" in the present or "succeed" in the
sense that today's world understands success. It does claim

to be the only way of getting the present translated into the glorious future that God has prepared for it.

Arcane (Hidden) Discipline

The above suggests that Christian ethics will be forced into a somewhat different approach than is customary. Certainly in the case of the new morality and in that of many earlier ethical systems as well, Christian thinkers have attempted to provide a moral code and a rationale that would appeal to and apply to Christians and non-Christians equally. This option is not open to the ethic of promise.

Of course, Christian ethicists still will have an obligation to speak to the world which God loves, to offer and teach to the world as high an ethic as it can accept. But an ethical system based upon a promise that the people have not heard, calling men to venture toward a reality they do not see, will never make sense and cannot be expected to make sense to a secular world. Evangelism (the speaking and hearing of the good news which is the promise of the kingdom) is the prerequisite of the ethic of promise.

This is to say that it is an ethic of the church (in the broadest sense of the term "church") and that it will not fit in any other context. It is an "arcane discipline" in the sense in which the earliest Christians used that term; it is a demand but also a source of strength, which is hidden from the eyes of the world precisely because it is a secret wrapped in the gospel promise not yet accepted by the world.

A Trial Run

The ethic of promise will have to be given much more specific application than I have done thus far. As a starter, and for purposes of comparison, it might be fun to use one of Joseph Fletcher's favorite illustrations regarding the new morality. However, before bringing in the ethic of promise, let us write a few more chapters in the Fletcher mode. We may need to modify a few details for our purposes but will change nothing that affects the ethical delineation of his story:

A woman imprisoned in a concentration camp is desperate to get out so that she can care for her hungry, homeless children. A guard offers to help her escape if she will submit to his lecherous advances (in Fletcher's story there was a regulation that the camp would dismiss her as a liability if she were found to be pregnant, which the guard helped her to become). She does the right thing—in Fletcher's book—makes her escape, and has no regrets.

Let us write a second chapter. The woman is out of the camp but still several hundred miles from her children. The time is winter, and she, of course, is without resources. Unless she gets some food her earlier "sacrifice" (Fletcher calls her stratagem "sacrificial adultery") will have come to nothing. A farmer offers to give her food if she will (you guessed it!) submit to his lecherous proposition. If her previous action, motivated by a loving concern for her children, was right, so obviously is this. She submits and is fed. But she can't walk all the way home; she would freeze to death. A trucker offers her a ride if . . . No guilt was involved earlier; why now?

When finally she arrives at the city near the village where her children are, the woman suddenly realizes that a mother will be of little use to them unless she can provide for them in some way; clearly, it would be more loving to feed them than simply to starve with them. Enough lecherous propositioners are around to enable her to raise a bankroll and so fulfill the goal for which she sacrificed her way out of prison. She submits; no regrets. Finding these sacrifices not too onerous, she continues, hoping to accumulate still greater funds so that she can demonstrate still greater love . . . only to discover that she has become such a person that the most loving thing she can do for her children is to stay away from them.

Granted, I have reduced Fletcher's example to absurdity —but at what point did it become so? At which proposition should she have started to feel guilty? My story is consistent with Fletcher's rationale—and it is no more rare or far out than many of the examples the new moralists come up with.

But now let us go through that story again, this time under the rubric of the ethic of promise rather than that of the new morality. The woman is given the opportunity to buy her freedom and be reunited with her children. How does the promise of the kingdom relate? Obviously, in the kingdom women will not have to submit to adultery, sacrificial or otherwise. And by God (read that literally), they don't have to now! God has promised, and his promise is not some dream for which one sits around and waits; it is a promise upon which one *acts,* acts as though it were coming true, acts so as to allow it to come true.

Certainly such heroic refusal could prove costly. It may be that the mother is called to sacrifice her own freedom and perhaps the very lives of her children. (Here, by the way, is the true meaning of "sacrifice," not Fletcher's bail that gets one out of the clink and home to the kids.) But some people are going to have to volunteer to pay the price—as God already has paid and is paying the price— if the kingdom ever is to become reality. What would have happened to the promise in the early church if all the Christians who were needed at home had chosen to perform the sacrificial adultery of burning the incense?

What would be the positive consequences of the woman's refusing to compromise the promise? Who knows! Some lechers might get a new insight into what women can be. Upon hearing the story, the woman's own children (and other women's children) might catch something of the mother's faith and be inspired to some heroism of their own. The woman herself might find life's richest blessing in losing her life for the kingdom. It has happened before! Above all, the God of Promise (the God whom the new morality largely ignores) dare not be overlooked when we calculate the consequences. No one can predict what he may choose to do—even in an earthly, physical sense—for and with those who dare to live according to the promise. But in any case, the woman's act is predicated not on how it will pay off in the present but on whether it points toward God's future.

Nothing New

One disadvantage of the ethic of promise is that it never can be billed as something "new"; it is too close to the biblical. . . . I take that back; it could be called the New *Testament* morality. Perhaps it nowhere is better summarized than in one little petition from the Lord's Prayer. A number of authorities now are convinced that more accurate than the translation "Give us this day our daily bread" would be "Our bread for tomorrow give us today." And, of course, if the Father, who has promised this bread and to whom we address the petition, proceeds to give such bread, he expects the recipients to eat it and to live off it. And that, no matter how you slice it, is the ethic of promise.

This article brought to the Century *the following letter, which in turn moved me to clarify my thought and make a response.*

SIR: It was an enjoyable experience to watch from my grandstand seat as Vernard Eller administered the *coup de grâce* to Joseph Fletcher's cavalier equation of murder, adultery and the like with "the good" pure and simple—in certain circumstances. But if I may, I shall step into the arena for a moment to ask a question of Mr. Eller: Can we apply the kingdom ethics to our broken, fallen situation in the absolutist fashion you suggest? Your illustration is compelling ("In the kingdom women

will not have to submit to adultery, sacrificial or otherwise.
And by God they don't have to now!"). It is less compelling when other terms are substituted: "In the kingdom
we will not have to fight poverty and disease, and by
God we don't have to now!" Or, "In the kingdom we
will not have to forge I.D. cards to save Jews from
Nazis, and we won't do it now!"

I believe that Helmut Thielicke provides a corrective
for both Fletcher and Eller. He recognizes that there
are kingdom standards (which Fletcher does not), but
(contra Eller) he sees situations wherein these must
reluctantly and regrettably be set aside in order to serve
God and our fellow men. At the same time he insists
that we pray and hope for the day when deceit and
murder will not be required in order to show neighbor
love—as will certainly be true of the kingdom.

WILLIAM S. SAILER

SIR: . . . [The ellipsis indicates that the *Century*
editors cut out one of my cute remarks; where the Doubleday editors have done it, no ellipsis will appear.] William S. Sailer questions whether the kingdom norm I
proposed in "The Ethic of Promise" can be applied as
absolutely as I suggested.

In the first place, I certainly never meant to imply
that the little formula I used on Joseph Fletcher is the
absolute. The kingdom of God cannot be reduced to a
neat equation.

Second, I did not mean to imply either that to use the
kingdom of God as an absolute norm immediately makes
all ethical decisions easy, obvious, and clear-cut. There
are no magic answers in this realm.

Third, even with the kingdom norm the Christian still
has to use the brains God gave him. I submit that
Sailer's first try—"In the kingdom we will not have to
fight poverty and disease, and by God we don't have
to now!"—isn't even a sincere and honest one. The

New Testament makes it as plain as day that God in Christ was and is fighting against all the enemies of man and that the kingdom comes precisely as such powers are put under his feet. Obviously the formulation should be: "In the kingdom there will be no poverty and disease, and by God we can begin to clean those pests out now!"

Sailer's second attempt is much more to the point: "In the kingdom we will not have to forge I.D. cards to save Jews from Nazis, and we won't do it now!" This is a fair application of my principle, but at this point I would not go along with Thielicke in reluctantly and regrettably setting aside the kingdom norm. That I see as a very dangerous step. What principle is to control this presumptuous setting aside of one's normative principle? What is to keep it from sliding into a setting aside whenever it suits whim or convenience?

No, I would rather put alongside Sailer's formulation another one of equal validity: "In the kingdom there will not be some people persecuting and exterminating other people, and by God we should prevent that from happening now!" Here we have *two* statements of the kingdom principle—both valid—and yet we seem to face a particular situation in which human sin makes it impossible to be obedient to both. Where this eventuality arises the person must decide which action (either of which will involve both obedience and disobedience to the kingdom norm) will be of greater service to that kingdom.

This procedure may bring one to the same choice Thielicke would make; but mine, I feel, is the safer route. Far from being set aside, the kingdom principle (i.e., "Which action will be of greater service to the kingdom?") not only is retained but is used to guide the decision.

VERNARD ELLER

2

I Can't Give You Anything But Love

———◆———

The new morality bases its whole pitch upon LOVE. The ethic of promise shows no desire to argue the point but suggests that in the Christian gospel "love" does not stand as an independent, self-sufficient concept but as an aspect of a much broader picture. If an ethic is going to claim to be contextualist it had better start by asking whether it has love itself in proper context. And we are going to contend that, according to the New Testament, the very idea of love is eschatological, i.e., end state oriented.

Underlying the new morality seem to be some rather largely unexamined assumptions. In the first place, it is assumed that people automatically know what love is. It is true that some of these moralists translate love back into the New Testament Greek word *agapē*. Theoretically, that gets everything right; if men were to practice what the New Testament understands as *agapē*, morality *could* stop with that; no further guidance is needed. The hang-up is that most people haven't the foggiest notion of what the gospel means by *agapē*—and the new moralists aren't for much in helping them find out.

In the second place, the new morality assumes that most people, by nature, *want* to love—or to put it as strictly as the case demands, *want* to practice *agapē*. Or perhaps it would be more accurately put to say that the new morality points its appeal to man's inherent drive to practice *agapē*.

But what if it is the case that something first must *happen* to a man before he even has such a desire? Then, of course, morality must go back a step and take care of that little matter before rushing into its exhortational challenge, "Get in there and LOVE!"

In the third place, the new morality assumes that if a person *wants* to practice *agapē* he can go do it. As simple as that! Why not? What's to stop him? But what if it should be that human beings don't have what it takes? What if *agapē* should turn out to be more than a man can hack— even if he is smart enough to see what it demands? In such case, the morality that counsels "Go, love!" is of little help until it speaks to the problem of wherewithal.

The biblical understanding of *agapē,* we maintain, is big enough to face and deal with the difficulties we have just raised, whereas the new morality simply grabs the word "love" and tries to jump over them.

This leads us to a point that was touched upon in the *Century* article, and which we will need to pursue in a later chapter, but which demands attention here. The new morality is not actually a *Christian* morality.

I mean that statement for what it says, but I do not mean it as judgmentally or self-righteously as it probably sounds. At stake is a matter of fact rather than a value judgment. Within the total context of the New Testament it is plain that the injunction to love, to practice *agapē,* is directed to *Christians*. And Christians here are understood not simply as men who believe thus and so, but men to whom something has happened that makes them radically different. In short, the full word of the Bible is: "Be converted [in the sense in which a coal stove is 'converted' to gas, i.e., get remodeled to where you can burn *agapē*] and then you *can* love!"

The new morality does take its love command from the New Testament, but obviously it does not take along this prior premise; it is not all that discriminating in whom it addresses. The exhortation to love is splashed all over the

place—in the secular media as well as in the churches—and
without any consideration that the mass of hearers might
be constitutionally unsuited for such counsel. The new morality speaks the last word of the gospel without speaking
the first word. It assumes that one moral scheme can apply
to Christian and non-Christian alike; and thus it is not, in
the final analysis, a *Christian* morality. Of course, it may be
a more-than-Christian morality—if it can bring off its implied program of leading even non-Christians to a Christian
level of morality. But that is a very big "if."

The ethic of promise, on the other hand, is explicitly
Christian and makes no sense on any other grounds. It accepts the Christian presupposition that something radical
must happen to a man before he is capable of attaining
the truest sort of morality. Thus it will not blare out the
admonition "Start cooking with gas!" without first giving
attention to the design of the stoves involved. A central
aspect of its contextualism is the context of the gospel; it
is an ethic for Christians.

With this, we are courting a serious misunderstanding.
We will deal with it in detail later but must make some
attempt to head it off now. Are we implying that morality
can spring only from Christianity, that only Christians have
the possibility of being moral? No, we are not saying this.
But secular men and men of other faiths necessarily will
live by systems of morality that grow out of and are con-
genial to their own commitments and beliefs. Obviously
Christians believe that their faith provides the best grounds
for the highest order of morality, but that is not to deny
that other men can reach greater or lesser levels of moral
achievement through other approaches.

Of course the Christian's prime hope is that his fellows
will themselves accept Christianity and thus become eligible
as practitioners of *Christian* morality; yet we shall consider
whether even a Christian moralist has not the possibility
and even responsibility for offering ethical instruction and
guidance that can apply to non-Christians. But the ethic

of promise is not offered as this sort of help for the masses;
it is a gospel ethic for those who have accepted the gospel.

We have made free in criticizing the way other people
have defined (or failed to define) *agapē*. We now are on
the spot to come up with something better.

There are several different alternatives open to us as we
decide *how* to get at *agapē*—as there are with other problems as well. For example, while walking across campus
(I am a college professor) I meet a stranger who asks me
how to get to Founders Hall. I *could* tell him: "Go south
on this sidewalk past the library to the sidewalk that runs
along the north side of Third Street; turn right until you
come to the crosswalk; take it and continue across the sidewalk on the south side of the street; proceed straight ahead
along the divided sidewalk and up the broad steps to the
main entrance of Founders Hall." But I would never do
that. I would point and say, "There it is!"

If someone who happened not to know were to ask me
how to walk, I *couldn't* tell him. I know that it must have
something to do with tensing certain muscles and relaxing
certain others, but the act of walking is too complicated (or
perhaps too simple) for a mind like mine. I could *show*
him—and in fact already have demonstrated my compe-
tency by doing just that for my children.

In this regard the Bible is my kind of book. Realizing
that *agapē* is too complicated (or perhaps too simple) for
a mind like mine, it does not attempt the matter with defi-
nitions, verbalizations, conceptualizations, and all such; it
is content to point and to show.

The Bible's first word on love is not that of the new
morality, the command to "Go, love!"; it is the pointing
exclamation "God loves!" You want to know about *agapē*?
Watch him do it—even *feel* him do it! At spots the Bible
does condescend to talk a little about how a person who
has *agapē* acts, but it makes no pretense of coming up

with a definition which would have the effect of domesticating *agapē* into a concept.

The key to the biblical approach is a verse from the First Letter of John: "In this is love, not that we loved God but that he loved us and sent his Son to be the expiation for our sins" (4:10). And a few verses later when the author says, "God is love" (vs. 16), this is not an attempt to define God by forming a direct equation between God and *agapē*. Neither is it, strictly speaking, an attempt to *define* love. It is a pointing to the spot where one can see love for oneself: "There it is! What God *does* is what love *is!*" *Agapē* is not theoretical and cannot be theoretized; it only can be seen and experienced—and that pre-eminently where *God* is doing it, for it is his invention, his very own thing.

So it is what God does! But what, pray tell, does God do? John, in his own pointing, was willing to be more specific than simply "Behold, God!" What God does, he specified was to send his Son to be the expiation for our sins. You want to see God doing *agapē*? Look at Jesus—and particularly his death on the cross—and know that this is God giving his Son for the sake of others.

Here is the proper focus of the matter, but there is more that must be said, especially since we have not yet begun to get eschatological. So, what (even more specifically) was God doing in giving his Son on behalf of others? We can be helped in answering that question if we realize that this, although God's outstanding effort, was by no means the first time he had been known to practice *agapē*. Indeed, it was because men already had seen something of it that they were able to recognize the death of Jesus as being God in his *agapē*. So what is it that God does and has been doing whenever and wherever he does *agapē*?

In creating Adam (and a world for him), in calling Abraham out of Haran, in leading the children of Israel out of Egypt, in making the covenant at Sinai, in anointing David king, in as many such events as you care to enu-

merate, what God was doing was establishing his kingly
rule among men. And God's "kingly rule" is what the Bible
signifies with the phrase that usually is translated "the kingdom of God." ("The kingdom of heaven" is the same ideo-
gram, preferred by pious Jews who did not want to dis-
honor God by speaking his name with their sinful lips.)
What God does in each of his mighty acts and pre-eminently in the giving of his Son is to lead humanity toward
that day when his kingdom shall come and his will be done
on earth as it is in heaven. And what God is doing when
he does this *is agapē; agapē* is activity which serves to
further God's kingly rule among men, which serves to advance mankind toward the situation in which God's will is
universally and in all respects the order of the day.

Let us dig in a little on this "kingly rule," or "kingdom,"
of God; it is an idea (more than an idea, a reality) with
which we shall be dealing throughout this book and which
is essential even to our understanding of love.

If *agapē* is something not to be defined but to be pointed
out, so much the more so is the kingdom of God—it is
a reality that is not yet even present (at least in its totality)
but is a promise and hope *of the future*. The kingdom of
God has to do with God's grand scheme for the world, his
ultimate intention for this race of men he created in his
own image and over which he has agonized and labored
so long, his dream about where the great drama we call
history is to come out. It should be plain that a matter of
this scope and "futurity" is not to be "defined" or compre-
hended (i.e., boundary-staked) by the mind of mortal man.
To the extent we even try that, to that extent we miss the
kingdom *of God* and get a kingdom *of man* in its stead—
and they are not the same thing.

Although at points some of the biblical writers use a
phraseology and imagery that may sound like a rather detailed description of the kingdom, closer study will indicate
that they rather are using picturesque and imaginative language precisely to hint at and point toward that which de-

fies human definition. The biblical effort is to be understood as men opening themselves to whatever God has in store and not as getting a jump on the future by figuring it out ahead of time.

However, this insistence on letting the king himself both define and establish his own kingly rule is not to suggest that we can say nothing whatsoever about the kingdom. After all, "pointing" is itself a way of saying something. And although the kingdom in essence is a future and thus a "not yet," it is also a funny sort of future that is sufficiently "already" that it can be pointed to in the here and now.

Modern scholarship has made it clear[1] that the biblical phrase "the kingdom of God" is not a reference to *a place*. This is why the translation "kingdom" is misleading; we use the word so geographically that we can speak it without any thought of the ruler or the quality of his rule. But in the Bible the reference is precisely to the fact and character of God's ruling and, secondarily, to the order, the situation, that is created by that rule. Not only is it impossible to consider the kingdom apart from the king, the kingdom is nothing more nor less than the kingly activity of that king—the kingdom is the king in his kinging. (Do you sense the convergence between *agapē* and "the kingdom of God" that this line of thought will make possible? Both are concerned with what God *does*.)

The kingdom in no sense is a "where." Because it is so much an *activity* of God, it hardly qualifies as a "what." The what involved is that of our world and us men, this history which constitutes human existence. The kingdom essentially is a "how," *how* this world is going to be; but the words "going to be" make it primarily a "when." It does not take much knowledge either of God or of the world to know that that when is not yet; if God's will, his kingly rule, actually were the order of the day, a lot

[1] For a scholarly opinion that does have the advantage of being clear, see Gerhard Gloege, *The Day of His Coming* (Philadelphia: Fortress Press, 1963), pp. 137ff.

of things would be a lot different than they are now. Obviously, men, devils, and no telling what other critters presently are resisting the kingly rule of God.

So the kingdom of God is a when, a future, a new age, the age to come, "that day" (as the Bible puts it). All this is true, but there is more that must be said; it cannot be correct to imply that God's kingly rule is entirely absent in the here and now. After all, he did create the world and presumably it still is at least something like what he intended. Presumably, too, at least some men in some things some of the time do what God has in mind for them. In short, the natural world itself displays obedience as well as resistance to God's kingly rule.

Further, the Bible claims a whole series of events as being steps taken by God in the process of bringing humanity under his kingly rule. Perhaps the record's first such act is his making clothing for Adam and Eve, an effort to undo the shame they had brought upon themselves by defying God's kingly rule. But a more classic example is God's promise to Abraham: "Go from your country and your kindred and your father's house to the land that I will show you. And I will make of you a great nation, and I will bless you, and make your name great, so that you will be a blessing. . . . and by you all the families of the earth will bless themselves" (Genesis 12:1–3). In other words, "What I will do here with you is a step toward bringing all men into the kingdom." God's kingly rule now is far from complete, but it is being actively exercised and pursued—and in a way that points toward its ultimate consummation.

But the Christian gospel, when it comes along, goes a whole step further in proclaiming the presence of the kingdom. Its basic announcement is that in the sequence of events which God has been performing in the establishment of his rule he now has reached and executed the one that *achieves* it. "Achieves" we do not intend as synonymous with "completes." A given touchdown, a goal-line stand, or even a fumble recovery can be said to *achieve* a football victory quite some time before the gun, the final score, and the switch from tackles to handshakes signals it *completed*.

This "crux event" is, of course, Jesus Christ. And it is not coincidence that the coming of the kingdom focuses on the same event that the John author claimed as the focus of *agapē*; God's loving of men is a purposed activity, and that purpose is the establishment of his kingly rule. But this Jesus, according to the New Testament, is both the inaugurator of the achievement and the proclaimer of the imminence of the kingdom. More, he is himself a visitor from the kingdom, a sample of the kingdom, an end-state man present before his time. More still, rather than being simply "sample," he is "first fruits," the *one* who brings in his train the *many* of harvest. He will "come again" as the agent of the end, but even now those who identify with him, who come to be "in him" (to use the Apostle Paul's favorite expression), in this very act are with him brought under the kingly rule of God and into the new age. By thus entering the kingdom these men receive not simply a new rule and ruler, but in light of *who* that ruler is they experience new powers, new possibilities, new privileges, new blessings.

This is the gospel proclamation and invitation, yet it is made in such a way as never for a moment to deny the essential *futurit*y of the kingdom. The Christian, more than other men, is painfully aware of the gap, the immense distance that obtains between the present world order and what the kingly rule of God promises for the future. He finds this gap within himself as well as in society at large. And he feels the width of the gap precisely because in his Christian experience he also has felt intimations of the gap closed.

Christian doctrine, then, demands a concept of "the overlap"—the present age of man (in his alienation from God) overlapped by the future age of God (in *his* kingly rule). The idea has been given a vivid if not quite adequate meta-

phor by D. E. H. Whiteley.[2] It is, he suggests, as when
a man comes out of the cold into a warm room; he still
feels the cold of the old age which is passing, but he also
feels the new warmth of the kingdom which is coming to
be. The analogy starts fine; in Jesus Christ, God has provided the warm room which the Christian enters through
the commitment symbolized in baptism, there to experience
the overlap of old cold versus new warmth. The difficulty
comes at that point; the "shift of the ages" takes place so
imperceptibly that the man cannot say at what point the
cold world disappeared and God's warmth became all in
all. But the Bible will not sustain such a "fade"; it stakes
its hope on another mighty act of God, a "return" of
Christ, an *eschaton* (the Greek word for "end") which will
be as dramatic an event of new creation as the first creation
was in its time.

What the New Testament has in mind has been no better
understood than by J. R. R. Tolkien—and that in his
faërie opus *The Lord of the Rings* (of all places!). That
trilogy has to be read for the sheer enjoyment involved;
but once done, it is permissible to derive a little theology
from the experience as a sort of fringe benefit. The move
is legitimate; Tolkien is a devout Christian who translated
the Book of Job for the Jerusalem Bible.

In a 1938 lecture on fairy stories, Tolkien made the
point that any great work of the genre must have a happy
ending and, more particularly, a sudden, surprise turn from
disaster to glory. He coined a word to express the idea:
eucastastrophe. "Catastrophe" is a Greek word meaning
"overturning." We use the term for what strictly should be
called a *dys*catastrophe, a dive into *evil*. But Tolkien wants
to speak of the alternative that happens so seldom that we
don't have a word for it, a spring into joy. (C. S. Lewis,
a close friend of Tolkien's, may even have extracted his
beautiful title *Surprised by Joy* from the brain of this master

[2] *The Theology of St. Paul* (Philadelphia: Fortress Press, 1964), pp.
126–27.

of faërie.) Tolkien, then, takes the "eu" from *euaggelion* (=*good* news=the gospel) to create *eucatastrophe*—a word which, if we had had it for the last two thousand years, might have made for a little *eutheology*.

Tolkien, who knows that the world's greatest fairy story was in fact the gospel truth, explicitly identifies the Christ event as being "the greatest and most complete conceivable eucatastrophe."[3] But he misses the heart of the matter on just one point. Clearly, the New Testament sees the Christ event as being the *penultimate* eucatastrophe that heralds and guarantees the ultimate eucatastrophe of the consummation of the kingdom of God.

Tolkien gets the whole matter straightened out, however, in *The Lord of the Rings*. (I am not suggesting that that story is a Christian allegory; it is not an allegory at all; it is its own thing, a "subcreation," but based upon the pattern that God originally invented for *his* creation.) The Powers of Evil threaten to inundate the whole of Middle-earth. If Sauron, the Dark Lord, can get possession of the One Ring which is of the very focus and stuff of evil, the means of total victory will be his. By chance, however, the Ring is held by a very ordinary little hobbit, one Frodo Baggins. The Ring dare not be held (it corrupts the holder though he be the best of creatures). It cannot be hidden (Sauron has the means of locating it). It must be destroyed (and the only way that can happen is by its being thrown into the volcano where it originally was forged, which volcano lies in the heart of Mordor, Sauron's own realm). After three volumes, untold sufferings, the very narrowest of squeaks, terror on every side, and dyscatastrophes enough for the history of a world, Frodo does get the Ring into the volcano. Eucatastrophe then is the word; Middle-earth is saved; Sauron disappears; and I saw a new heaven and a new earth.

But the economy of this eschatology is the crux of the

[3] See "On Fairy Stories" in *The Tolkien Reader* (New York: Ballantine Books, 1966), pp. 68–73.

matter. There can be traced a sort of progress toward the kingdom; Frodo is, in one way or another, getting the Ring closer to the volcano. But on the other hand, the sheer fact of the approach both brings Frodo farther into Sauron's territory and excites Sauron's powers of interception. The closer the story brings us to the *possibility* of salvation, the less seems the *likelihood* of its happening. And just so with the kingdom of God. There is a progress; an approach is taking place; men here and now have a responsibility and an assignment regarding its coming. And yet gradual fulfillment is not the answer. Christians, as Frodo, know that it will take a eucatastrophe to bring the matter to success. But Frodo lives—and, without benefit of buttons announcing the fact and despite theologians who would have it otherwise, so does the One the thong of whose sandals Frodo is not worthy to untie.

The Bible wants both a dramatic consummation at the end (resistance to God's kingly rule is simply too deeply engrained in the world to imagine that it will just gradually evolve out) and a very real overlap in the present. With my college students I have tried a different analogy to get at the matter. Our semester has an eschaton; the catalogue specifies that at 4:00 P.M., Friday, January_____, the first semester is over, kaput, done and gone, and that the new, kingdom-of-God second semester takes the scene as of that moment. Any papers, projects, and exams not completed by that hour miss it—without excluding the possibility that there is a professorial grace of God that can operate even in such desperate eventuality, although one ought not count on it. I urge, too, that my students live as men of this world, unmindful of an overlap or even an age to come; the first semester provides enough to keep them busy—with all those papers, projects, and exams. But with me, as professor, the case is different (I try always to design my analogies so that I get to be the Christian). By virtue of the fact that I am professor (as the Christian, by virtue of being in Christ, has been raised with him into the life of the new age) I have the prerogative, the where-withal, and the responsibility to live in two semesters at once. I cannot escape the first semester; after all, those papers, projects, and exams must be graded. Nevertheless I cannot wait until the eschaton to start the second semester; sometime before the demise of the first I must be ordering textbooks, organizing schedules, making class plans, and all such—dealing with the second semester as a very real and present bit of business. The professor, as the Christian, is a busy man; but, as the Christian, he wouldn't want it any other way (although I will admit a slight romanticization in the implication that he enjoys grading papers, projects, and exams). But in any case, the eschaton is still as real and significant for him as for anyone; an overlap need not negate the possibilities of an eschaton.

The Bible's unique and interesting concept of a time overlap is crucial to the ethic of promise and to the entire argument of this book. It means that the present and the future cannot be thought of as independent of one another or even as simply sequential. Because of what he has done in Jesus Christ, God's kingly rule of the future is breaking into the present, the kingdom even now is actualizing itself, the end (no matter when God may choose to consummate it) is at hand. Under these terms, then, to live for the future is not to engage in the irrelevancy of pie in the sky by-and-by but to deal with the most germane aspect of the present. Under these terms, to live simply for the present is the greatest possible irrelevancy, for the truest thing that can be said about the present is that it is the current installment of God's future. Under these terms, the future, rather than being simply the undetermined "not yet" of which we can make whatever we will when the time comes, is the source, locus, and determination of God's kingly rule both now and when. It has been promised by One who is faithful; it is "achieved" in Jesus Christ; it can be lived in even today.

According to the ethic of promise, the end (*telos*) of

ethical endeavor is the establishment of the kingdom of God (the kingly rule of God). But the case is not that I envision that end and then devise a means for moving toward it. In the first place, I am not God (nor, I make so bold as to suggest, are you), and what I would envision as the kingdom of God sure as shooting would turn out to be something other than the kingdom *of God*. In the second place—still not being God—the means I would devise for getting us there wouldn't get us *there* in the first place. No, the "means" to *the kingdom of God* is to become obedient, radically obedient, to *God's kingly rule* in the present. Amazing coincidence—and amazing grace! In this case—if in no other within the whole of creation—there is no possibility of ends and means getting out of whack, for both amount to the same thing. (In a later chapter we shall speak of the *power* of God that guarantees the end even when the means seem completely inadequate to accomplish it.)

Eschatological perspective, the establishment of God's kingly rule, is the context of the entire Bible; an *overlap* eschatology (the future which is "already" even as it is "not yet") is the context of the entire New Testament. The very concept of Christian love (*agapē*) derives from this context and divorced from it is no longer *Christian* love. The sin (I use the word advisedly) of the new morality is not in staking everything upon love but in emasculating love by tearing it away from its roots and secularizing it.

"God is love"—what *God* does is what love *is*. "In this is love, not that we loved God but that he loved us and sent his Son to be the expiation for our sins"—and what God does in his loving, and what he did particularly in Jesus Christ, is to move men into the future of his kingly rule, the most loving thing that can be done for anyone. And all this says a great deal about the nature and character of *agapē* love.

In the first place, because it comes out of an eschatological context, love itself takes on an eschatological aspect; it is activity which is oriented toward an end-state goal, toward the long-term—yes, even ultimate—future. And if love is of this character, then it simply will not fit into immediate situations in the way that the "situationalists" attempt to do it. The new morality tends to assume that situations and their consequences are compact, self-contained, independent, and discrete—so much so that one is encouraged to make his moral decisions in the moment on the basis of the immediately foreseeable consequences for the immediate participants. But if love is eschatologized as its gospel context demands that it be, then it can be applied only as the situation is broadened out to relate to humanity as a whole and lengthened out to reach even to the kingdom of God.

In the second place, if love is what God does in moving mankind toward the kingdom, then love is not primarily a *feeling*. Of course, it is safe to assume that when God *acts* toward man as he does, he also *feels* loving toward man in the process, and the Bible so indicates. The feeling of love *may* even be the motivation for acts of love—although we must not preclude the possibility that love can be active even where the feeling is not present. When, for instance, Jesus enjoins us to love our enemies, is he asking us to come up with certain *feelings* toward them? I am not sure that our feelings are all that much at our beck and under our control.

Although certainly it would be wrong to belittle either the value or the sheer pleasure of feelings of love, the quality of the feeling dare not be made the determination of what is love and what is not. Feelings are about the most transient and undependable things people have, and some of the most atrocious acts ever perpetrated on human beings have been done by those who "felt" loving. Indeed, some prize examples come even from those who "felt" motivated by a holy love for God. Jesus recognized the eventuality: ". . . the hour is coming when whoever kills you will think he is offering service to God" (John 16:2). Even the famous and worthy saying "Love God and do what you please" is dangerous until the content of "love God" is rather critically examined. To assume, as the new morality tends to do, that natural man naturally knows what love is and so can play it by the seat of his pants, by glands not far removed therefrom, or even by "the heart," is an insult to the gospel; God's great act would have been superfluous if "in *this* is love, not that he loved us and sent his Son, but that we proceed according to our loving feelings."

By attempting to recover the eschatological setting in which Christian love belongs, the ethic of promise moves the emphasis away from love's "feeling" component to the nature of its "activity" and provides some norms by which the activity can be tested as to whether or not it is of love. *Agapē* love is *activity,* like God's, which serves to bring men under his kingly rule and into his future.

We have striven to find for love a content that gives some guidance as to what acts are loving and what are not, but Christian love demands a dimension that goes entirely beyond this. Men are not pointed to God simply that they might learn of him and then go out and do it on their own; that the end of love is God's *kingly rule* has the effect of keeping him deeply involved throughout. Our John author can help us again here: "We love, *because* he first loved us" (1 John 4:19). The total impress of the passage makes it clear that he is saying much more than that we now can love because we have *seen* God do it. If to be loved by God means to experience his kingly rule, then in being loved by God I also have been released from and forgiven for some hang-ups which effectively have prevented me from being a lover; I have discovered a source of power, guidance, and transformation that only now makes true loving a possibility. It makes sense that only one who recognizes God's kingly rule and himself has experienced something of it is fully capable of helping others toward it. Or to put the matter even more strongly, yet in a way the gospel would support: If the love you would practice is to be Christian *agapē*, then it can be done not by your initiating love but only by your becoming a channel through which God's love can operate. Most certainly, in the final analysis, God's kingly rule can be established only through God's kingly power.

So there is nothing in the world wrong with the new morality's staking everything upon love; it *has* failed to look very deeply into what love is. The ethic of promise marks an attempt to overcome that deficiency.

3

A Tale
of Three Cities

The home of the new morality is the Secular City. It is the ethic designed and fitted especially for men of that city. The two phenomena came on the scene almost simultaneously, and they belong together.

It was, of course, the book by Harvey Cox that gave us the picture of the Secular City, celebrating its liberties and inviting us into its disciplines. However, he was not responsible for the new morality that now goes with it; and there is evidence that he didn't even intend the city as being quite all that secular. Our discussion, then, is not meant to focus upon Harvey Cox but upon the entire "secular theology" binge of which the new morality is part and parcel.

In the theological context of the new morality, Cosmopolis (the city of this world, which is the Secular City) is the eschatological equivalent of what Theopolis (the city of God) is in biblical thought. Our "city" metaphor is nothing more than an attempt to compare and contrast the eschatological perspectives of the new morality and the ethic of promise.

The what-could-be-called "eschatology" of secular-city thinking gets to where it does through a chain of ideas that runs something as follows: the Secular City=Technopolis (the city of modern technology)=Cosmopolis (the city of this world)=the City of Man=the City of God=the New Jerusalem (Revelation 20–22).

The weak link here is the one that connects the City of
Man with the City of God. Yet this is precisely the transi-
tion the secular theologies make as the man who now has
come of age prays, "Father, I would rather do it myself!"
This is the thrust of today's new humanism; in order to
ascribe to man the freedom, responsibility, dignity, and
power which are felt due him, God gets downgraded. It
cannot be denied that neither God, his activity, nor his
power figure very prominently in the new morality—which
is what we meant earlier in suggesting that it is not actually
a *Christian* morality.

However, the ethic of promise—within its context of the
theology of hope—does not attempt to counter this secular
move by resisting the thrust toward humanism; quite the
contrary! Rather, it sides with Kierkegaard in his statement
that Christianity is the only true humanism. Man does not
find his truest humanity by fighting free of God but precisely by committing himself to God. Man does not get up
by putting God down; neither is up until both come up
together. This was the entire argument of my earlier book,
His End Up (Abingdon, 1969).

The proponents of the Secular City, then, really ought
to defend their equating of the City of Man with the City
of God and give reason why the following chain of the
Bible should not rather apply: the Secular City=Babel=
Babylon=Rome=the Great Whore="Was there ever a
city like the great city? Alas, alas for the city, the mighty
city of Babylon! In a single hour your doom has struck!"
(Revelation 18:18, 10 [NEB]).

It often has been pointed out that the beginning of this
biblical chain (where Cain is named as the builder of the
first city and wherein is described the blasphemous pile of
mud brick and bitumen which God had to come down from
heaven in order even to see) expresses a primitive nomadic
aversion to urban culture. Be that as it may, it ought not
be forgotten that the Yahwist, the writer who gave these
stories their theological import by incorporating them into

redemptive history, was no nomad but a sophisticated citizen of Solomon's Jerusalem, as close a model of the Secular City as Israel ever achieved.

It is very true that the Bible itself describes and supports a move toward secularization, but we dare not assume that every movement that goes under the name merits biblical approval. The world of the Bible was a world chock-full of gods, spirits, totems, taboos, priests, shamans, and what all, conspiring to tyrannize man and bind him tight with fears, guilts, and religious prescriptions. In came Yahwism (the worship of the God of the Old Testament), making free to rip out this whole religious apparatus—secularize it—so that Yahweh might be left standing high as the one true Holy about which life could be organized.

The modern move toward secular theology has been impelled by something of the same worthy motives, i.e., the desire to fight free of the stultifying and dehumanizing effects of "religion." Yet one rather significant little detail has been overlooked. The biblical strategy was that, at God's initiative, every "holy" *except Yahweh* be brought low in order that his true holiness might stand high and sovereign. The modern strategy seems to be that man, at *his own* initiative, desacralize *everything* so that Man the Secularizer might be left standing high. It is proper that Religiopolis, the city of "religion," be attacked—or at least deserted—but it does not follow that the Secular City is *the* place (or the only place left) to go. The biblical commentary on the Secular City dare not be so quickly skipped over.

A long time ago now the Bible knew all about Religiopolis and provided the motif-chain to describe it: Religiopolis=Jerusalem=The Holy City=Zion="The temple of the Lord! The temple of the Lord! The temple of the Lord!" (Jeremiah 7:4)="Look, Teacher, what wonderful stones and what wonderful buildings!" (Mark 13:1)= "The hand of the Lord was upon me, and brought me in the visions of God into the land of Israel, and set me down upon a very high mountain, on which was a structure like a

city opposite me. . . . 'And you, son of man, describe to
the house of Israel the temple and its appearance and plan.
. . . This is the law of the temple: the whole territory
round about upon the top of the mountain shall be most
holy. Behold, this is the law of the temple.'" (Ezekiel
40:1-2; 43:10, 12).

The Bible knows about Religiopolis, but that is not to
say that it approves. We traced the biblical chain that opposes the Secular City; here is the one that opposes Religiopolis: Religiopolis=Jerusalem=The Holy City=Zion
="Do not believe in deceptive words. . . . I will do to the
house which is called by my name as I did to Shiloh."
(Jeremiah's wording of God's response to the temple-of-
the-Lord religionists—Jer. 7:14)="Do you see these great
buildings? There will not be left here one stone upon another, that will not be thrown down." (Jesus' response to
his religion-tempted disciples—Mk. 13:2)="I saw the holy
city . . . [but] I saw no temple in the city." (the New
Testament revelator's response to the religious prophet
Ezekiel—Rev. 21:2, 22).

The secular theologies are right in proclaiming that Religiopolis is marked for destruction; the Bible says as much.
However, the Bible does not so much as hint that Cosmopolis is the city of the future to be reared in its stead.
Quite the contrary, Cosmopolis is itself just as surely
marked. It is a third city in which the Bible invests its
capital, Theopolis, the city of God. Its motif-chain climaxes:
Theopolis=the *New* Jerusalem="The first heaven and the
first earth had *vanished*. . . . 'Behold, I am making all
things *new!*' . . . For its temple was *the sovereign Lord
God.*" (Revelation 21:5, 22 [NEB])="the city which
has foundations, whose builder and maker is God" (Hebrews 11:10)="Have no fear, little flock; for your Father has chosen to *give* you the kingdom." (Luke 12:32
[NEB]).

Here we have moved into the true eschatological context
of the gospel. Theopolis is not Religiopolis; the *New* Jeru-

salem is not the old, religious Jerusalem under a program of urban renewal. The Religiopolitan civic center, the temple, is gone forever and not missed. Theopolis is not built out of man's religious pieties—nor out of his secular heroisms. Rather, the word is that it is the all-new construction of the builder and maker (although not by that token done without man's involvement), who pleases to give it to his little flock. But at least Theopolis is the New *Jerusalem* and not the New Babylon—that city disappeared two chapters earlier (in Revelation 18) and "shall be found no more." The City of God may well be a city *for* men, but it is not the city *of* Man—not the city of Religious Man, and, if possible, even less the city of God-ignoring Secular Man.

Our discussion thus far has proceeded under rather etherealized symbols. Yet almost by accident as it were, the three-city theme has been given a very much down-to-earth, historicized explication. *The Day of His Coming* (Fortress Press, 1963) is an exciting study of Jesus written by Gerhard Gloege, a scholar who lived in East Germany at the time of the book's writing. The book opens with an intensive analysis of the world into which Jesus came. Gloege's basic assertion, convincingly argued, is that the Judaism which formed the background to the day of Jesus marked a high point of religiosity at the very same time that Hellenistic-Roman culture was marking a high point of secularity.

One very striking implication is that Religiopolis and Cosmopolis are not nearly as antithetic and incompatible as the secular theologies would suggest. They can and do coexist very nicely. In fact, many men can and do so compartmentalize their lives that they can dwell in both cities simultaneously. Indeed, if basically religion signifies man's attempt to control God, to pipe in his blessing and power for our own convenience, to dictate to and influence him for our own ends, then to go totally secular is nothing more than the ultimate act of religion. To ignore God, or even to declare him dead, settles once and for all the issue of who is in control of whom. Thus it is not a question of *either* Cosmopolis *or* Religiopolis; they are twin cities—Sodom and Gomorrah, if you will.

But Gloege's main point, of course, is that both the world of acute religiosity and the world of acute secularity were under judgment, that both were in dire need of a Savior, that Jesus came to save men out of the one no less than the other, that his salvation was a promise of and an invitation into the kingdom of God, which is Theopolis. And whether or not it is true—as the secular theologies and new morality would have it—that twentieth-century man has come of age and moved out of Religiopolis into Cosmopolis, what should be clear is that the move would be nothing gained, for in the twentieth century (as in the first) not religiosity or secularity but only Christianity will avail now and prevail at the day of his coming.

It may seem as though we have drifted rather far from our assigned task of doing ethical analysis, but that is not the case. We have been considering eschatological alternatives (or perhaps alternatives to eschatology), but it is out of these that our alternative ethical systems also grow. If it is contextualism the new morality wants, it is contexts we shall supply. Now we are exploring *theological* contexts.

Religiopolis inevitably produces authoritarian, priest- or book-dictated ethics of codified prescriptions. "God's word" —which certain men and institutions claim to possess, along with a divine license to transmit, interpret, and enforce it—is used to bully people, regiment them, deny their personal standing before and access to God. To a real extent (although probably not as completely as the new morality would like us to think) the Christian church had drifted into Religiopolitan modes. There was abroad a dehumanizing legalism that deserved protest and rebellion. Thus there was nothing at all wrong with the new morality's call to freedom; it was justified, and we can thank God for it. The question, however, is whether Cosmopolis actually is the free city it is claimed to be.

Although it has gone by different names at different times, the new morality is the regular brand of Cosmopolitan ethic. Its emphasis—naturally enough, in view of what it is revolting against—is *freedom.* There is no law but love; within that broad limit all is permitted, each person is free to find his own way. And so there obtains a humanism which sees man as essentially right-minded, competent, trustworthy, and responsible. Each man is his own moralist.

What we propose, then, under the name of the ethic of promise, in no sense is to be understood as a defense of Religiopolis or criticism of the new morality's leave-taking. We are at one with the new morality in desiring to get free of Religiopolis, but we would make so bold as to point out that Cosmopolis is not the only place to go, that homes also are available in Theopolis. Thus ours is an attempt at a Theopolitan ethic—although no more of a new invention than the new morality is.

The basic issue at stake, as rightfully has been seen, is *freedom,* the freedom for persons to become truly human. Our three cities represent three radically different concepts of freedom. And although our "city" metaphor is not used, perhaps the greatest ever discussion of these three concepts of freedom is Fyodor Dostoevski's story of the Grand Inquisitor.

Kenneth Hamilton already has used the Grand Inquisitor for a critique of the new morality (*The Christian Century,* December 4, 1968), but if I may express an opinion, I think I see that Dostoevski sees more than Hamilton sees he sees (give or take a few "sees"). But be assured that I am not copying from Hamilton, although one could do worse; my ideas were on paper before I saw his article.

Any reader who does not avail himself of the opportunity to read the story of the Grand Inquisitor is missing the best part of this book. The story is found tucked within the novel *The Brothers Karamazov,* but it also often has been published as a separate item.[1]

Essentially, Dostoevski's story is a debate between secular humanism (Cosmopolis), represented by Jesus (actually, as we shall see, by the Inquisitor's *idea* of Jesus), and the church (Religiopolis), represented by the Inquisitor. The issue at stake is precisely that raised by the new morality, namely the value, role, and possibilities of human freedom. Neither side comes off well at all, and the whole encounter is most frustrating. Yet a careful reading makes it evident that this is just what Dostoevski intended. The *tertium quid* of the Christian gospel (Theopolis) is not presented, although Dostoevski drops enough hints to reveal that he knows it is there. Clearly, Dostoevski intends to make the reader commit himself; if he accepts the argument on the Inquisitor's terms and allows the choice to be forced between Cosmopolis and Religiopolis, he "is condemned already, because he has not believed" (John 3:18).

The conclusion, which Dostoevski does not here state but toward which he only pushes the reader, he did make explicit upon another occasion. From his Siberian imprisonment he wrote: "Freedom is an inward movement of the heart to something ultimate." There is here a great paradox, that *freedom* is to be found in an act of commitment or submission, which is what a "movement of the heart to something ultimate" must denote. And as Dostoevski's story makes clear, it is precisely the inability to master this dialectical movement that dooms both religiosity and secularity. In Religiopolis, "submission" is well enough emphasized, but the "something ultimate" is claimed for an ecclesiastical hierarchy and/or an authoritarian code. To ascribe ultimacy to that which is not ultimate is idolatry, and it produces, not freedom, but its very opposite. On the other hand, in Cosmopolis, with its new morality, "love" is exalted as the "something ultimate" (although whether

---

[1] The quotations that follow are from the translation by Constance Garnett (Liberal Arts Press, 1948).

anything resembling "submission" is involved is highly questionable). However, as was suggested in our previous chapter, this "love" has been detached from the true ultimate, which is God, his will and purposes, to become in effect "doing what my good instincts tell me is best under the circumstances." Thus "self" has been made the idol, and what Dostoevski makes so graphic is that this idolatry destroys true freedom just as surely as ecclesiastical idolatry ever has done.

The story—which in the novel is told by Ivan to his brother Alyosha—is that Jesus appears on the streets of Seville at the height of the Spanish Inquisition of the fifteenth century. Immediately he is apprehended and imprisoned by the dedicated old cardinal who is the Grand Inquisitor. Then, late at night in the privacy of the cell, the cardinal comes to argue why it is that, for the good of mankind, the religious tyranny of the church rather than *what he understands to be* Jesus' gospel of a new, free humanity must hold sway and why, therefore, Jesus cannot be allowed to return to earth.

At first blush it would seem as though the debate is between the Grand Inquisitor and Jesus; on second thought, it is clear that such is not the case. Jesus himself says not one word in the entire story; the Inquisitor states his case for him. Dostoevski goes out of his way to call attention to this fact by having Ivan say, "He comes on the scene in my poem, but He says nothing, only appears and passes on." A hint of this sort ought not be simply passed over, for now the debate actually is not between the Inquisitor and Jesus but between the Inquisitor and his own concept of Jesus—an entirely different matter!

That Dostoevski intended the distinction is indicated by three crucial clues:

(1) Ivan's portrayal of Jesus and the people's response to him before he is captured do not reflect the same viewpoint that the cardinal's words do.

(2) Most important is the little key exchange in which

Ivan interrupts his story to suggest that it is out of love
for humanity that the cardinal had rejected Jesus and joined
the hierarchy, the religionists, i.e., "the clever people."

> "Joined whom, what clever people?" cried Alyosha,
> completely carried away. "They have no such great
> cleverness and no mysteries and secrets. . . . Perhaps
> nothing but atheism, that's all their secret. Your in-
> quisitor does not believe in God, that's his secret!"
> "What if it is so! At last you have guessed it. It's per-
> fectly true that that's the whole secret. . . ."

But Dostoevski's secret goes much deeper than simply
revealing a certain cardinal of the church to be an atheist.
Although he is not accusing the entire citizenry of Religiopolis and Cosmopolis—the practitioners of both ec-
clesiastical-authoritarian morality and the new morality—
of being self-conscious atheists, he is implying that in
neither of these moralities is the presence of an active, ef-
fectuating God a necessary part of the picture.

It must be borne in mind that because the Inquisitor is
an atheist, his understanding of Jesus is based upon the
same presupposition; his is a secular Jesus, the Christ of
Cosmopolis, decidedly not the Jesus Christ of the New
Testament. God is not necessary to the Inquisitor's own
"religious" morality; all that is required is the name of
God, with which the church can cow the masses into obedience. But neither is God necessary to what he understands
as the "Jesus" morality; once the teaching of love has been
put into circulation, men need only accept and practice
it. Dostoevski means what he says in suggesting that "the
whole secret" of his story is that God is left out, and it is
crucial to note that the possibility of a living God never
comes into consideration in the Inquisitor's debate.

(3) The final hint that the Inquisitor's presentation of
Jesus is not to be identified with Jesus himself comes at

the conclusion of the story as the Inquisitor finishes his condemnation of Jesus and sends him away:

> He saw the Prisoner had listened intently all the time, looking gently in his face and evidently not wishing to reply. The old man longed for Him to say something, however bitter and terrible. But he suddenly approached the old man in silence and softly kissed him on his bloodless, aged lips. That was all his answer.

Here, in the one communication that comes from the real Jesus rather than the Inquisitor's understanding of him, as plainly as can be done, Dostoevski has him say, "Father, forgive them, for *they know not what they do.*" No matter how brilliant or well-intended the debate between Religiopolis and Cosmopolis, until Theopolis is in the picture the truth has not been told; until God has been made Lord, all possibilities of human freedom are illusory.

The debate between the Inquisitor and his Jesus, between Religiopolis and Cosmopolis, does not come out in favor of the new morality. Jesus' gospel of a humanity freed to discover and live out of its own "situational" ethic, freed to love according to the impulses of its own good heart, is condemned as unrealistic. The Inquisitor's entire argument is staked on the proposition that the mass of men are not good enough, wise enough, disciplined enough to use and preserve their freedom; turn man loose and you get anarchy and the terrible tyrannies it creates; the last state is worse than the first.

> "Thou [Christ] mayest not take from men the freedom which Thou didst exalt when Thou wast on earth. . . . The freedom of their faith was dearer to Thee than anything in those days fifteen hundred years ago. Didst Thou not often say then, 'I will make you free'? But now Thou hast seen these 'free' men. . . . For fifteen centuries

we have been wrestling with Thy freedom, but now it is
ended and over for good.

"Instead of taking men's freedom from them, Thou
didst make it greater than ever! Didst Thou forget that man
prefers peace, and even death, to freedom of choice in
the knowledge of good and evil? Nothing is more seduc-
tive for man than his freedom of conscience, but nothing
is a greater cause of suffering. And behold, instead of giving a firm foundation for setting the conscience of man
at rest forever, Thou didst choose all that is exceptional,
vague and enigmatic; Thou didst choose what was utterly
beyond the strength of men, acting as though Thou didst
not love them at all—Thou who didst come to give
Thy life for them! Instead of taking possession of
man's freedom, Thou didst increase it, and burdened the
spiritual kingdom of mankind with its sufferings forever.
Thou didst desire man's free love, that he should follow
Thee freely, enticed and taken captive by Thee. In
place of the rigid, ancient law, man must hereafter with
free heart decide for himself what is good and what is
evil, having only Thy image before him as his guide.
But didst Thou not know he would at last reject even
Thy image and Thy truth, if he is weighed down with
the fearful burden of free choice?"

There would seem to be little if any difference between
what the Inquisitor here describes as Jesus' morality and
what we know as the new morality. His judgment is that
it has not worked and cannot work; most men simply do
not have what it takes. The Inquisitor makes his case as
Dostoevski presents a most remarkable exegesis of the
Gospel account of Jesus' temptation in the wilderness.
Satan urged Jesus to "take possession of man's freedom"
and direct it through the instrumentalities of *miracle* (feed-
ing the masses with rocks transformed into bread), *mystery*
(casting himself from the pinnacle of the temple without

harm), and *authority* (taking over the kingdoms of this world). Jesus, of course, turns down the proposal—and this, the Inquisitor is convinced, spelled the failure of Jesus' mission. Because Satan's understanding of human nature was so much more accurate in this instance, the church (in the name of *Jesus* and out of a true love for humanity) has had to take up the very instrumentalities which Jesus himself had rejected. Obviously, in the Inquisitor's eyes, the worst thing that could happen would be for Jesus to come back and undo the "saving work" of the church.

The Inquisitor's argument is powerful and convincing indeed—much more so than our poor description of it can be. It would be most enlightening if some of our modern moralists would be forced to show any defect or give reason why his case does not apply to today's new morality. The Inquisitor's own option is to insist that because the mass of men are incapable of handling freedom, the elect few who are capable must create an ecclesiastical god (a church/law regime) through which these men can be controlled for their own good. The proposition very seriously is presented that it is a greater act of *Christian love* to help men by ruling them than to send them to damnation by turning them loose with the mere counsel that they love one another. Even so, unless there is a third alternative (and by God, there's *got* to be!—as Dostoevski himself was the first to realize), we are forced to consider whether our escape from Religiopolis into Cosmopolis may not be a descent into hell.

The Inquisitor's argument was good enough to convince (and thus trap) a man who would be expected to be a supporter of the new morality—and perhaps was. The eminent British novelist and man of letters D. H. Lawrence wrote a commentary on Dostoevski's story.[2] Lawrence himself was not enough of a Christian to catch Dostoevski's

[2] "A Preface to Dostoevsky's *The Grand Inquisitor*" in *Dostoevsky: A Collection of Critical Essays,* ed. by Rene Wellek (New York: Prentice-Hall, 1962), pp. 90ff.

hints about the possibility of the third alternative, so he assumed that the Inquisitor's is a true picture of Jesus and that the Inquisitor speaks for Dostoevski. Thus he concludes:

And we cannot doubt that the Inquisitor speaks Dostoevsky's own final opinion about Jesus. The opinion is, baldly, this: Jesus, you are inadequate. Men must correct you. . . . Man can but be true to his own nature. No inspiration whatsoever will ever get him permanently beyond his limits. And what are the limits? . . . The limits are, says the Grand Inquisitor, three. . . . Man on the whole makes three grand demands on life, and cannot endure unless these demands are satisfied. . . . These three demands, for miracle, mystery, and authority, prevent men from being "free." . . . Only a few men, the elect, are capable of abstaining from the absolute demand for . . . miracle, mystery, and authority. These are the strong, and they must be as gods, to be able to be Christians fulfilling all the Christ-demand. The rest, the millions and millions of men throughout time, they are as babes or children or geese, they are too weak, "impotent, vicious, worthless, and rebellious." . . . Is it true that mankind demands, and will always demand, miracle, mystery, and authority? Surely it is true. . . . Dostoevsky was perhaps the first to realize this devastating truth, which Christ had not seen. A truth it is, none the less, and once recognized it will change the course of history. All that remains is for the elect to take charge of the bread—the property, the money—and then give it back to the masses as if it were really the gift of life. In this way, mankind might live happily, as the Inquisitor suggests.

In these words Lawrence aligns himself with the most totalitarian sort of "religious" morality; but when one puts what he says here against his own life and work, the question arises as to whether he did not consider himself one of "the elect," those who are "as gods," who are capable of handling the freedom of the new morality. I wonder if the promoters of the new morality would buy Lawrence's thesis that theirs is a morality of the elect who are as gods? And if this is what the hippies, the beautiful people, the playboys—all the most prominent practitioners of the new morality—represent, I for one choose to identify with "the rest" who are "babes or children or geese." Lawrence raises even more problems for the new morality than Dostoevski does.

Human freedom must be considered from *three* perspectives, the perspectives of the three cities. Cosmopolis gives us the Inquisitor's secular understanding of Jesus. If the possibility of transcendent help or power is ignored, then the freedom that Jesus proclaims is *autonomous* freedom, freedom *from* God rather than *for* God. Man has come of age and is on his own, completely responsible for what he is to make of himself and of his world. But, Dostoevski and the Inquisitor maintain, man simply does not have the wherewithal to sustain himself in autonomous freedom; autonomous freedom inevitably deteriorates into man's slavery to his own finiteness, weakness, selfishness, ignominy, and sin. Thus what in theory would appear to be the greatest possible freedom shows itself in actuality to be the worst sort of slavery.

The Religiopolitan alternative is what the Inquisitor sees in his role as administrator of ecclesiastical law. If man is not capable of autonomy, then religion must step in and rule. The church practices a benevolent tyranny for man's own good; through his higher slavery to the church and religious ideology man is rescued from autonomous slavery to himself. Human fulfillment is to be found not in freedom but in slavery of the right sort.

But consider the third alternative, that of Theopolis and the ethic of promise. Dostoevski only hinted at its existence as the source of true freedom. Søren Kierkegaard has best explicated it; he knew what Dostoevski was getting at—

even though the Dane wrote his commentary *before* the Russian wrote his novel. I have used this quotation in each of my earlier two books and now use it again. I shall continue to use it until I find something better—or until some publisher blows the whistle.

> The most tremendous thing which has been granted to man is: the choice, freedom. And if you desire to save it and preserve it there is only one way: in the very same second unconditionally and in complete resignation to give it back to God, and yourself with it. If the sight of what is granted to you tempts you, and if you give way to the temptation and look with egoistic desire upon the freedom of choice, then you lose your freedom. And your punishment is: to go on in a kind of confusion priding yourself on having—freedom of choice, but woe upon you, that is your judgment: You have freedom of choice, you say, and still you have not chosen God.[3]

In one sense D. H. Lawrence is right: "Man can but be true to his own nature. No *inspiration* whatsoever will ever get him permanently beyond his limits." But what if it were the case that, when a man uses his freedom to choose *God,* this were the opening for God to bring him under his kingly rule, into the coming age of the New Creation in which man is resurrected into a *new* nature that does precisely "get him permanently beyond his [old] limits"? Then, bound to God, man would be free both from the tyranny of his sinful self and the religious tyranny of miracle, mystery, and authority.

As Kierkegaard said: "There is only one way: . . . give it back to God, and yourself with it."

As Dostoevski said: "Freedom is an inward movement of the heart to something ultimate."

[3] *The Journals of Kierkegaard,* trans. and ed. by Alexander Dru (New York: Harper Torchbooks, 1959), p. 189.

As the Gospel of John has Jesus say: "If the Son makes you free, you will be free indeed."

And to complete the circle to where we left off in the previous chapter: What God does when he *loves* men is to bring them under his kingly rule and when a man comes under that kingly rule he finds *freedom*. What a man does when he loves another man is to help him into the kingly rule of God where *he* can find *his* freedom. Both love and freedom are eschatological gifts; both are found in Theopolis; and this is the ethic of promise.

4

On Whose Authority?

———◄•◆•►———

What we started out to talk about was love. What we are trying desperately to get back to talking about is love. But in ours, as in so many other cases that start with love, one thing leads to another.

We had to deal with eschatology. That got us involved in secularity and religion; and these in turn led to a discussion of freedom. Somewhere we need to talk about authority. It is a tossup as to whether it should be done here or later when we come to a consideration of the relation between love and law. But because Dostoevski's story is so germane, "here" gets the toss—with the understanding that the next chapter will deal directly and exclusively with love.

The New Testament understanding of love ties in closely with its understanding of authority; the two must go together. In the first place, it should be noted that "authority" and "authoritarianism" are not the same thing—at least in my book they aren't (and this, it so happens, *is* my book). Henceforth "authority" and "authoritative" shall be good words; "authoritarianism" and "authoritarian" their evil counterparts; "author" (namely me) shall remain neutral.

An "authority" is one who is sufficiently knowledgeable in a subject that his opinions can be accepted on face value as being accurate. At my college, for instance, we have a professor who is an authority on marigolds—on that unpretentious, foul-smelling, little weed flower, the marigold. He devoted his doctoral dissertation to their study. And because I know that when it comes to marigolds Bob is the authority, I never bother to question or check out what he says; I simply accept his word as the truth. Before the subject of marigolds even comes up I know that he is much more qualified than I ever will be—or than I have any desire to become. In one sense my relation to him is that of "blind faith"; I do not have the wherewithal to test what he says, although I do have sufficient evidence to know that his is an authority in which I can put confidence.

In the final analysis, however, even Bob is not *the* ultimate authority on marigolds. The ultimate authority, I suppose, would be the consensus obtaining among the several researchers of his caliber. Even so, the possibility would have to be kept open that in the future, through the progress of research, there might arise a consensus even more authoritative than any currently available. As regards marigolds, then, the concept "ultimate authority" must remain somewhat relative. However, when we say (as we are going to in a bit) that God is the ultimate authority on love, this relativity disappears. God being who he is and love being his very own invention, what he understands love as being is what love is—there is not even the possibility of it being any other way. Of course, we still are left with a question as to who speaks for God or how his authoritative interpretation of love is communicated to us; nevertheless it is undeniable that the Christian faith proclaims an authoritative view of love. Too seldom, however, does the new morality bother to point men toward any authority beyond themselves.

"Authoritarianism," on the other hand, we take as designating a fake, bogus, imitation, illegitimate authority. It speaks a word that claims to be authoritative but which does not have the credentials to back it up. And because authoritarianism is not authentic and at heart knows that this is the case, it manifests a basic insecurity. This insecurity customarily shows itself through actions which we know as "authoritarian"; it is pushy, self-assertive, coercive; it tends also to be glib, noisy, blustering, arrogant. What it does not have in its own right, authoritarianism must give the show of having.

Conversely, because true authority *does* have what it takes, it feels no need of resorting to show. It is secure in the knowledge of its own credentials. True authority doesn't have to use bluster to make its point; it is self-authenticating. You don't have to listen to my professor friend talk marigolds for very long until you *know* that he knows what he is talking about. When anyone would dispute it, true authority is secure enough in its own authenticity that it doesn't have to get all hot and bothered in defending itself. It can afford to be "defenseless," to let the opposition blow itself out—which, we shall see, is itself one of the hallmarks of Christian love.

Quite the contrary, authoritarianism always is frantic to line up everyone according to its point of view, exerts strong pressures toward conformity. Dostoevski's Grand Inquisitor makes a very good picture of (and case for) authoritarianism—even an authoritarianism sincerely designed for the good of those it would rule. But while authoritarianism gets frantic, true authority is willing to let time take its course, confident that its truth ultimately will have the victory.

As Dostoevski well understood, there also is a correlation between freedom and authority. The Inquisitor represents an ecclesiastical authoritarianism, namely some men taking it upon themselves to run the lives of other men, telling them what is right, what is good, what is permissible. The question is whether any man or group of men actually have credentials qualifying them to exert this sort of power over others—and it is this consideration that makes necessary the distinction between true authority and authoritarianism. But in any case it is clear that authoritarianism is itself an abrogation of human freedom; by their very natures, authoritarianism and freedom are incompatible.

The obvious option, then, is that represented by the Inquisitor's misunderstanding of Jesus. Here is a position that renounces all authority in the interests of freedom. It would seem to follow that if *authority* (although we will contend that the word should be "authoritarianism") marks an abrogation of freedom, then the rejection of authority would have the effect of maximizing freedom. However, the point of the Inquisitor's very effective argument is to show that this does not follow. Indeed, quite the opposite; the rejection of authority marks the *loss* of freedom. My rejecting of authority is in effect to presume authoritative status for myself; I am now my own authority. But it can be questioned, as the Inquisitor does so tellingly, whether individual men have the competence, the credentials, to be their own moral authorities. Dostoevski, the Christian gospel, and a great deal of human experience would say, "No, they do not." And if this judgment is accurate, then it is the case that man simply has chosen another sort of authoritarianism, self-authoritarianism, which is every bit as prohibitive of freedom as any external authoritarianism can be.

It is not *authority* that is a threat to freedom; *falsehood* is. The only way of being free is by being in the truth, and authoritarianism is an abrogation of freedom because it is not of the truth. True freedom, however, can come only in finding true authority. It is amazing, for example, to what degree my relationship to Bob Neher makes me free in regard to marigolds. I am completely free and feel so. I do not have to lie awake nights worrying as to whether my knowledge of marigolds is adequate. I do not live in fear that the day may bring a marigold crisis that I will not be able to handle or that I inadvertently have treated marigolds in a way that will bring unhappy repercussions. Knowing a marigold authority does make me free in relation to marigolds—and although the illustration may not be too apt, the principle is entirely valid: To find a true authority is truly to find freedom.

We live in an age that is in revolt against authoritarianism. The statement is self-evident; there is no reason even to attempt to substantiate it, because anyone inclined to argue the matter wouldn't be reading this book in the first place. And to the extent that it is a revolt against *authoritarianism* this revolt is all to the good; God knows that we have set up all sorts of bogus authorities which, in the name of truth, need to be thrown out. It is nothing less than calamity, however, when the distinction between authority and authoritarianism fails to get made and the revolt becomes a throwing out of true authority along with the false. When this happens, the fight for freedom has overshot its mark to wind up in a libertinism which becomes about as unfree an existence as men can invent for themselves. And that the current revolt in many instances has gone to this extreme is almost as self-evident as the fact that there is a revolt going on.

The new morality represents one sector of this revolt; it cannot be understood except as a reaction against authoritarian moralism as it has come to pervade much of society's and particularly the church's teaching. The revolt was justified here as in many other aspects of cultural and political life. At the same time it must be said that the church probably never was as guilty of authoritarianism as the new moralists make it out to be; it is understandable that the rebels would tend to overstate the case in their own favor. Yet to the extent that society and the church have been guilty of such moral authoritarianism and to the extent that the new morality is aimed at correcting the situation, to that extent it merits our sympathy and support.

The question that must be asked, however, is whether in the interests of its entirely valid struggle against authoritarianism the new morality has not lost sight of the

necessary role that belongs to true authority—whether in
its entirely valid struggle for freedom it has not thrown off
one authoritarian oppressor only to come under the oppression of self-authoritarianism. In any case, a central
feature of our ethic of promise is that it focuses upon
God as the moral authority in whom alone true freedom is
to be found.

It is quite evident that both the Christian gospel and
the teachings of the historical Jesus were founded upon a
concept of authority—and that this concept extended to
the matter of *love* as well as to all other matters of the
New Testament.

As certain as we can be regarding anything about the
historical Jesus, modern scholars tell us, is the fact that
"authority" was a central mark of his person and teaching.
Time after time, in what undoubtedly is accurate recollec-
tion, the Gospels report that "he taught as one having
authority."

Even more convincing is a slight stylistic innovation
which seems to have been original with Jesus. The customary procedure of the rabbis and other Jewish teachers
was to make a statement or give a teaching and then
append to it the little prayer "Amen," "Let it be so," or
"May it be so!" However, in instance after instance Jesus
is reported as employing a different, a unique usage. He
says, "Amen, I say unto you . . ." (This semantic twist
is hidden in most English translations of the Bible in that
the original "amen" is translated as "truly" or "truly,
truly.") Scholars agree that this wording must have been
authentic with Jesus and that it must have had particular
significance or it would not have been retained in the
memory of the early church. By using "amen" to open
rather than close a remark, Jesus seems in effect to have
been saying, "I am qualified to say that it is so," rather
than, "Having said it, I hope now that it is so." Here is an
impressive claim to authority.

There is much other evidence that could be cited in this regard. Indeed, the entire theme of discipleship in Jesus' teaching constitutes a claim to authority.

It is obvious also that the early Christians heard and accepted this claim of Jesus. Indeed, what was probably the earliest and most central Christian confession is the simple phrase "Jesus is Lord!"—nothing more nor less than a recognition of authority—"I accept him as the final authority on what my life shall be." In its bare essence, to become a Christian means simply to renounce my own wisdom and insight as authoritative for my life and look to God in Christ as my authority.

It should be said too that one also finds here all the marks of true authority as opposed to authoritarianism. In Jesus appears the ultimate in authority coupled with the ultimate in defenselessness. He could have had but did not need legions of angels to defend him, because his authority was securely of the truth. He could afford to go to the cross, because he knew that his cause was right and would prevail. There is nothing self-assertive, impatient, or coercive in Christ—or in God as he is seen in Christ. While it is true that there has been considerable authoritarianism in the church and in the *name* of Christ, there is not a hint of this in Jesus himself. He is, indeed, the very model of authority without authoritarianism.

And because we have not yet in this chapter so much as mentioned our thematic principle of eschatology, we had better make a point of doing so now. If human existence is essentially eschatological, i.e., end state oriented, then where man most needs the counsel of an authority is in that area where he himself is least adequate; he needs someone who can speak authoritatively about where existence is headed, where history is going to come out. And the only possible candidate for that job is God, the God who will be the Omega of creation as he was its Alpha and who is Lord of the whole. To go eschatological—which is the only way to fly—as much as demands a relationship to God the Authority.

Consider, finally, that if love itself is essentially eschatological, as earlier we maintained, it too must look to this authority. The upshot is that Christian love is "authorized" love—and that not only in the sense of being *permitted* or *licensed* by an authority but, even more, *directed* and *empowered* by him. Unauthorized love—in which the new morality tends to specialize—is not so much illegal as it is undependable, lacking as it does the wisdom, the power, yea, even the freedom of the authorized product.

Once a man—even a very ordinary sort of man—is "deputized" (i.e., commissioned by an authority) he is able to do a great deal in the way of making things jump, making people shape up, and even making heads roll— none of which he could do on his own, none of which *he* actually is doing now, seeing how he is simply the agent of a higher power which is the authority. Just so, to say that love is what God does is not saying merely that *our* loving is *like* what God does; no, when *Christian* love is the subject, then even *our* loving is *God's* doing it through us deputies. In our next chapter we shall let Robert Browning illustrate the point.

5

Pippa Passes—Cum Laude

Were it not for the publisher's petty qualm about helping an author get rich from somebody else's work, I would reprint Robert Browning's poem "Pippa Passes" (it isn't any longer than some two or three of our chapters). Yet, reprinted or not, there is no doubt but that the collateral reading suggestions are worth the price of this book.

Quite apart from what we intend to do with it, there is good reason for looking at "Pippa Passes." From this poem come the lines: "God's in his heaven— / All's right with the world!" And they are lines heard round the world, quoted by preachers as a flagrant example of the sort of shallow Pollyannaism that all true Christians—like the preachers themselves—are to deplore and desist from. It will be worth something to give the lie to these men—most of whom have never read the poem—and get in a lick toward redeeming the reputations of Pippa and Browning. The secret—to which we will get in due course—is that Pippa's affirmation is eschatological: Because God is in his heaven, all *is* in the way of coming right with the world. If it is permissible for Isaiah to say that the people who sat in darkness *have* seen a great light, when clearly he means that God's promise makes this future event as good as accomplished, then it is all right for Pippa to speak the same way without getting bad-mouthed from every passing pulpit.

The poem as a whole, however, is a most effective

demonstration of the thesis that "authorized" love is vastly superior to every other variety; and it is as such that we propose to use it. We need simply run through Browning's work, summarizing and commenting as we go along.

Pippa is a little orphan girl of Asolo, Italy, who makes her living (if that it should be called) in the silk mill. The entire poem takes place on New Year's Day, her one day of respite for the whole year:

> . . . Day, my holiday, if thou ill-usest
> Me, who am only Pippa,—old-year's sorrow,
> Cast off last night, will come again tomorrow:
> Whereas, if thou prove gentle, I shall borrow
> Sufficient strength of thee for new-year's sorrow.
>
> Thou art my single day, God lends to leaven
> What were all earth else, with a feel of heaven.
> (11. 30–35 and 39–40)

For all she knows, the one and only "good" Pippa possesses or can hope to possess is this day of freedom—if one can be called "free" who has no resources for enjoying his freedom. Let not this girl be coupled with those pampered ones whose ignorance leads them to believe that "all [everything, in fact and as it stands] is right with the world." Pippa's is a much more realistic faith than that.

She determines how to spend this, her day:

Tomorrow I must be Pippa who winds silk,
The whole year round, to earn just bread and milk:
But, this one day, I have leave to go,
And play out my fancy's fullest games;
I may fancy all day—and it shall be so—
That I taste of the pleasures, am called by the names
Of the Happiest Four in our Asolo!
(11. 107–13)

Pippa has the sense to understand that true happiness comes of being loved; and because she does not know herself to be loved of anyone (with a notable exception, as we shall see), her Happiest Four consist of those renowned in love.

> Some one shall love me, as the world calls love:
> I am no less than Ottima. . . .
>
> (11. 115–16)

Ottima and Sebald her lover represent the passion of sexual love—heterosexual love, it should be said (one dare take nothing for granted these days). Also, it is a forbidden, adulterous love. Browning betrays his Victorianism by putting this love at the bottom of his list, when any modern writer worth his salt knows it belongs at the top; it shows how far we had to come to get to the new morality.

So, in her fancy, Pippa moves up the scale:

> But love, love, love—there's better love, I know!
>
> For do not our Bride and Bridegroom sally
> Out of Possagno church at noon?
>
> (11. 127 and 130–31)

Jules and his bride Phene represent marital love—though it is strange, is it not, that we invariably think of this as something other than sexual love?

But Pippa's thought progresses:

> Lovers grow cold, men learn to hate their wives,
> And only parents' love can last our lives.
> At eve the Son and Mother, gentle pair,
> Commune inside our turret. . . .
>
> (11. 163–66)

Luigi and his mother represent filial-parental love. How long has it been since a new moralist has glorified this sort of love—or even given it notice?

Pippa goes one step further:

> Nay, if you come to that, best love of all
> Is God's; then why not have God's love befall
> Myself as, in the palace by the Dome,
> Monsignor?

(ll. 179–82)

The Monsignor, the bishop who is visiting Asolo, represents religious love; and the very implication that his being a monsignor guarantees that he is loved by God (or that he loves God) gives that word "religious" at least something of the negative tinge we encountered in a previous chapter.

Perhaps it is this very thought that brings Pippa to her deepest insight:

> Now wait!—even I already seem to share
> In God's love.

(ll. 187–88)

And at this point Browning has Pippa sing a hymn which is the crux of the whole poem:

> All service ranks the same with God:
> If now, as formerly he trod
> Paradise, his presence fills
> Our earth, each only as God wills
> Can work—God's puppets, best and worst,
> Are we; there is no last nor first.
> Say not "a small event"! Why "small"?
> Costs it more pain that this, ye call
> A "great event," should come to pass,
> Than that? Untwine me from the mass
> Of deeds which make up life, one deed
> Power shall fall short in or exceed!

(ll. 190–201)

The fact that Browning calls men "God's puppets" is enough to turn off modern readers; but hang on—that isn't quite what he means. His point is that any act done as a service to God is to be valued not for what the act accomplishes in and of itself, not for the results that follow automatically from the act, but for what God can make of it, what he can do through it. Men are to make of themselves instruments through which God can work beyond their own wisdom and power—not be "puppets" which *he* makes serve him against their own will.

Browning's thought is almost eschatological at this point. He does suggest that God is active in the world, working out purposes and goals of which men only dimly are aware, working in a way that is hidden enough that men cannot really judge which are small events and which great. The idea is one which in a later poem, "An Epistle . . . ," Browning makes explicitly eschatological.[1] But the basic point toward which he and we are driving is that love is what *God* does, that we do better as lovers by letting God work through us than by trying to be lovers on our own. Christian love is an "authorized" activity.

Already Browning has said some things worthy of note, but this is only the introduction to his poem; the body which follows gives demonstration to his theme.

Pippa hardly would seem to qualify as an outstanding lover. She has never experienced love—except the love of God. She does not look upon herself as particularly apt in loving; she hasn't anything in the way of resources or wherewithal. She does not even consciously set out to make a mark as a lover. Yet she turns out to be the greatest, becoming the means for both putting to shame and redeeming Asolo's Four Happiest. Her secret (a secret kept even from herself) is that she stays very aware of God's love for her and keeps herself open as a channel of that

[1] See my article, "Robert Browning: A Promising Theologian," *Religion in Life* (Summer 1969).

love. And although Browning does not put it so, it is plain that what God does through Pippa is to move men closer to his kingly rule.

The scene shifts to the finest villa in Asolo where the night is ending in which Sebald has murdered Luca, the senile husband, and possessed his beloved, the young wife Ottima. However, the reality of this desperately desired love is not coming up to expectation, and the lovers frantically are trying to invoke it, when Pippa passes by singing:

> The year's at the spring,
> And day's at the morn;
> Morning's at seven;
> The hill-side's dew-pearl'd;
> The lark's on the wing;
> The snail's on the thorn:
> God's in his heaven—
> All's right with the world!
>   (11. I:221–28)

The song from the street is heard in the villa. The reminder that there is a God in heaven and that his commitment is for the world to be right exposes the so-called love of Ottima and Sebald for the wrongness that it is. They know they are damned, but in that very damnation they discover, as it were, a truer, higher, a redeemed love. Sebald cries:

> . . . That little peasant's voice
> Has righted all again. Though I be lost,
> I know which is the better, never fear,
> Of vice or virtue, purity or lust,
> Nature or trick! I see what I have done,
> Entirely now! . . .
> I hate, hate—curse you! God's in his heaven!

As he moves to kill himself, Ottima responds:

> —Me!
> Me! no, no, Sebald, not yourself—kill me!
> Mine is the whole crime. Do but kill me—then
> Yourself. . . .
>
> (11. I:261–66 and 268–72)

Then, as both are dying, Ottima speaks the last words:

> Not me—to him, O God, be merciful!
> (1. I:282)

In Sebald was born a concern for right and truth, for God; in Ottima, a willingness to put the welfare of another above her own; in both, a perspective that looks beyond the moment to their eternal destiny and that of the world. And in this is love.

The scene shifts again; this time to the house of Jules, whose love is to be made happy this day as he becomes a bridegroom. It is quickly revealed, however, that the engagement and marriage are a cruel hoax. Jules is an artist who has run with a group of such characters; the picture is as close to a gang of hippies as Browning could come in 1841. Jules apparently was a rather arrogant fellow who somehow had offended one of his buddies, Lutwyche, and aroused his passionate hatred. To get revenge, Lutwyche had organized the gang for a devilish trick. They had located a beautiful but completely illiterate and uncultured peasant girl named Phene, bought off her protectoress Natalia, and established a correspondence between Phene and Jules—they writing the letters from her end. According to plan, Jules had fallen for her and proposed marriage. Now the wedding has just taken place, Jules still not having had face-to-face converse with his bride. He is entirely caught up in his love for her, and she—not

knowledgeable enough to realize what the true situation
is—responds with real love for him. However, the con-
spirators have drilled into her a rather obscure poem which
she is to recite to Jules and which will lead him to understand what has happened, who did it, and why.

Phene recites the poem, and Jules is disillusioned. His
first impulse is to give her all his money—that which he
had saved to finance a journey that would have ensured
his artistic career—desert her, and go forth to wreak
revenge upon Lutwyche and as many more of the gang
as he can lay hands on. But then Pippa, on her walking
tour past the homes of Asolo's Happiest Four, comes by,
singing. This time her song is a ballad, the lament of a poor
page who loved a queen but could find no way of expressing his love, because there was nothing he possibly could
do for her.

Jules hears the song and changes his resolve:

. . . If whoever loves
Must be, in some sort, god or worshipper,
The blessing or the blest one, queen or page,
Why should we always choose the page's part?
Here is a woman with utter need of me,—
I find myself queen here, it seems!

Now, to kill Lutwyche, what would that do?—save
A wretched dauber, men will hoot to death
Without me, from their hooting.

Who, what is Lutwyche, what Natalia's friends,
What the whole world except our love—my own,
Own Phene? . . .

(11. II:282–87, 301–3, 312–14)

He gives up his career to take Phene to her homeland,
there to live with her as husband and mentor.

And in this is love: to bear all things (even the hatred

and treachery of a Lutwyche); to seek not its own (but to give itself to one "with utter need of me").

As Browning shifts to the next scene, the turret in which dwells the third of Asolo's four happiest lovers (Luigi with his mother), we learn of a scoundrel and vagabond named Bluphocks who has been employed by Ugo, the bishop's intendant, to make an approach to Pippa—for what reason we are not told. Bluphocks also has been employed by a detachment of secret police from Austria to point out Luigi to them. It happens that Luigi is suspected of being a plotter in an Austrian freedom movement. He is to be watched; and the circumstances are such that, if he leaves for Austria on this very day, he can be assumed to be innocent and so let through. If he should leave at any later time, he is to be intercepted and taken into custody.

In the turret it turns out that Luigi is indeed a plotter and that he has planned an assassination which shall in fact free the nation from a terrible tyranny. However, his mother, out of love for him, tries to dissuade him from— or at least postpone—this dangerous adventure. She forwards his love for her as an argument against his going:

. . . Yet seems this patriotism
The easiest virtue for a selfish man
To acquire: he loves himself—and next, the world—
If he must love beyond,—but naught between.
(11. III:124–27)

And it is a temptation, is it not, to jump from self-love to great, broad, heroic nation-love, while skipping over the more mundane love obligations in between?

Luigi, who does truly love his mother, is wavering when (you guessed it) Pippa happens to pass by singing. Her song describes an ancient, legendary king whose justice, beneficence, and integrity were such that even an invading

python did not dare to assault him. Luigi hears the
song and speaks:

> The Python at the city, on the throne,
> And brave men, God would crown for slaying him,
> Lurk in bye-corners lest they fall his prey.
> Are crowns yet to be won in this late time,
> Which weakness makes me hesitate to reach?
> 'Tis God's voice calls: how could I stay? Farewell!
>
> (11. III:224–29)

He goes; and by going before the day is out presumably
ensures the success of his enterprise.

In a subsequent chapter we will seriously raise the question whether God ever wills assassinations and violence
against persons; but, granting Browning his presuppositions, this too is love—to risk and even sacrifice oneself
and one's more intimate loves for the sake of a broader love
of humanity.

As Browning shifts the scene to the last of the Four,
the bishop at the palace in which he has been installed
in Asolo, Pippa is told by some street girls who have
been put up to it that a handsome English gentleman
(Bluphocks, no less) has fallen in love with her and is
seeking to make her his wife and take her away to the
city. Pippa is not much interested.

The aged bishop, sick and near death, is making a final
visit to his family home in order to settle certain affairs. He
is in private conversation with Ugo, the intendant who had
been the right-hand man of the bishop's elder brother up
until his death some fourteen years before and who consequently had inherited from him a major share of the
family estates. The bishop knows that his kindred had
been rascals of the blackest sort and that Ugo was mixed
up in their monkey business. He is quite certain that Ugo's
getting the family property was a pay-off of some sort. He
suspects that his own second brother paid Ugo to murder

the infant child of the elder brother so that, instead of going to the child, the inheritance would come on down the line to where the second brother and Ugo could get at it. If the bishop can prove this allegation, Ugo will be convicted and dispossessed and the fortune will revert to the bishop and the church.

Ugo denies that the case is quite what the bishop believes but offers to make a deal. Ugo was not such a fool as to kill the child and thus open himself to blackmail and deprive himself of any bargaining power. The child is alive, unknown but accessible. If the bishop will let Ugo take an amount of money and flee the country, Ugo can see that the child is painlessly removed; the bishop will get his estates, and there will be no need to reveal anything of the whole sordid affair. Ugo assures the bishop that the child will not need to be murdered; in fact, he already has set in motion the machinery to take care of her. He has hired a certain Bluphocks to seduce her, take her to Rome, and involve her in a life of debauchery that will end her life in rather short order. The bishop seriously is contemplating the bargain when the girl herself (Pippa, of course) passes by singing.

Her song is that of a child who was just learning to appreciate the beauties of life and nature when "suddenly God took me." Hearing the song makes up the bishop's mind for him; he calls for his people to come take Ugo.

In this too is love—at least to the extent that love "does not rejoice at wrong, but rejoices in the right."

Pippa—completely oblivious to what has transpired among Asolo's four happiest ones and, for that matter, to what has happened to her own fortunes—retires to her barren room, where her closing words are:

Now, one thing I should like to really know:
How near I ever might approach all these
I only fancied being, this long day:
—Approach, I mean, so as to touch them, so
As to . . . in some way . . . move them—if you please,

Do good or evil to them some slight way.
For instance, if I wind
Silk tomorrow, my silk may bind
And border Ottima's cloak's hem.
Ah me, and my important part with them,
This morning's hymn half promised when I rose!
True in some sense or other, I suppose.

God bless me! I can pray no more tonight.
No doubt, some way or other, hymns say right.

> All service ranks the same with God—
> With God, whose puppets, best and worst,
> Are we: there is no last nor first.

(11. IV:280–96)

When it comes right down to it, perhaps we have not done much more than reprint Browning's poem after all—though perhaps it has been condensed enough that the publisher will let it through as being as much my work as Browning's.

It cannot be denied that there is a certain glib romanticism here—if the moral guidance of the poem is taken to be: Love God, wander around town singing whatever songs pop into your head, and trust Providence to take it from there. However, I am confident that this is not what Browning intended—and I know for a fact that it is not what I intend.

Certainly moral discourse must wrestle with knotty situations and issues and make some real tough determinations as to what is the most loving thing to do. And this book (if we ever get that far) is going to do some of that wrestling. Nevertheless, even morality's most competent wrestlers need to learn from Pippa; hers is the proper posture for wrestling as well as for all other forms of moral endeavor. Pippa, obviously, does not teach wrestling; she does demonstrate the proper approach to the mat.

Her word is that love is what we have called an "authorized" activity. That is, it is not based simply upon a human calculation as to what consequences the action will bring in the immediate situation. This is the way in which the new morality too often treats love. But human beings so easily get confused as to who are Asolo's four happiest lovers and what it is that qualifies them as such. Men on their own are not wise enough, good enough, strong enough, or farseeing enough to do a competent job of Christian loving. They need, therefore, to look to Love's Authority.

We then, as Pippa, first of all must remember that we have been and are loved by God. Next, with Pippa, we must learn to love *him* with heart, soul, mind, and strength. Third, as we turn to demonstrate this love to our fellow men, our pondering as to which is the truly loving action must be a conscious attempt to hear God's authoritative word rather than figure out our own answer. Fourth, we must be ready to be obedient to him even when the authorized action shows no promise of leading to the desired result; even when, as with Pippa, we can't foresee any results at all; even when it might seem as though the action would lead to adverse results. Finally, we must have Pippa's faith that "all service ranks the same with God," that even what we call "small events" can be used by him for purposes that go quite beyond our capability or knowledge. In short, we must love as under authority, under his kingly rule.

Within this process, of course, there is all the room in the world for the exercise of the best of human thought, study, energy, and dedication; the difference is that these gifts are directed toward discovering God's will and obeying it rather than toward an autonomous practice of what we choose to call love.

Pippa's lesson will be central to our thought through many of the ensuing chapters.

6

Two Loves Have I or Toward a Double Standard of Morality

———◆◆◆———

In one of my seminars at the college we read back-to-back, on successive weeks, Reinhold Niebuhr's *An Interpretation of Christian Ethics* and Søren Kierkegaard's *Works of Love*. For my money these are two of the greatest discussions of the Christian love ethic ever written. (It had not even occurred to me to ask the publisher to reprint them here; but they should go on our collateral reading list.)

However, treating them as I do always produces within me one grand frustration. Whichever book I am reading at the moment seems right, so very right. And yet, although they share many of the same presuppositions, they come to very different—actually incompatible—conclusions. Both can't be right; still, Niebuhr makes such eminently good sense, and Kierkegaard speaks so authentically like the New Testament. Finally (perhaps because I am getting at the truth of the matter but perhaps only because I must preserve my sanity) I am coming to believe that we have here two different Christian ethics, either of which is valid in its own sphere. At least that will be the case this chapter attempts to make: two Christian loves, a Niebuhrian and a Kierkegaardian, a double moral standard in all seriousness.

Although we are going to come out with Niebuhr closer

to the new morality and Kierkegaard closer to the ethic of promise, this is no good way to try to understand these men. For one thing, Niebuhr uses much more of explicitly eschatological language than Kierkegaard does—although, as you might guess, we will maintain that Kierkegaard's thought is more essentially eschatological than Niebuhr's. But in any case, Niebuhr cannot be classed as a new moralist—his analysis is much too profound and much of his extensive critique of liberalism hits too close to the new morality (even though Niebuhr wrote some time before the new morality was invented). On the other hand, Kierkegaard simply is not consciously enough eschatological to rate for the ethic of promise. Whatever correlation there may be between the two books and the two moral systems we have been confronting is very loose at best. We will do well to let both Niebuhr and Kierkegaard stand on their own feet.

Let us look first at Niebuhr's *An Interpretation of Christian Ethics*—although keeping an eye out for what Kierkegaard will have to say in his turn.

Time and again Niebuhr recognizes and uses the two different moralities which largely correspond to his thought and Kierkegaard's. However, to his way of thinking, only one of these is for real; the other is an ideal to keep the workable one honest.

The primary issue is how it is possible to derive a social ethic from the absolute ethic of the gospels. The gospel ethic is absolute because it merely presents the final law of human freedom: The love of God and the neighbor. A social ethic must be concerned with the establishment of tolerable harmonies of life, tolerable forms of justice and tolerable stabilities in the flux of life. (pp. 9–10)[1]

---

[1] All our quotations of Reinhold Niebuhr are from *An Interpretation of Christian Ethics* (New York: Living Age Books [Meridian], 1956 [first published 1935]).

The ethic of Jesus may offer valuable insights to and sources of criticism for a prudential social ethic which deals with present realities; but no such social ethic can be directly derived from a pure religious ethic. (p. 55)

Naturally, it is not easy to elaborate an adequate ethic for the immediate social problems of human existence in terms of the tension created by Christian love perfectionism on the one hand, and this kind of realism on the other. (p. 93)

No absolute limit can be placed upon the degree to which human society may yet approximate the ideal. But it is certain that every achievement will remain in the realm of approximation. The ideal in its perfect form lies beyond the capacities of human nature. (p. 104)

Niebuhr uses several different terms. Let us use "love perfectionism" to refer to the ethic which he also describes as being the ethic of Jesus (and perhaps, by implication, that of the New Testament as a whole), as absolutist, ideal, the final law of human freedom, etc. Likewise, let us use "realism" as our term to identify the ethic which he also calls prudential, tolerable, and which (note well) he almost invariably specifies as applying to "social" problems.

In order to discover how Niebuhr relates these two ethics we need to go somewhat deeper into his thought. As we do go deeper we discover that he has an impressive understanding of the role that eschatological perspective plays in Christian ethics. Reinhold Niebuhr *could* be quoted as though he had espoused the theology of hope and the ethic of promise thirty years ahead of its time. In going through his book for present purposes I was amazed to find so much of this emphasis—even though we later will consider the point that disqualifies him from membership.

High religions are thus distinguished by the extent of the unity and coherence of life which they seek to encompass and the sense of a transcendent source of meaning

by which alone confidence in the meaningfulness of life and
existence can be maintained. . . . The dimension of depth
in the consciousness of religion creates the tension between
what is and what ought to be. It bends the bow from which
every arrow of moral action flies. Every truly moral act
seeks to establish what ought to be, because the agent
feels obligated to the ideal, though historically unrealized,
as being the order of life in its more essential reality. . . .
Man seeks to realize in history what he conceives to be
already the truest reality—that is, its final essence. (pp.
17–18)

In genuinely prophetic religion the God who tran-
scends the created world also convicts a sinful world of its
iniquities and promises an ultimate redemption from
them. The realm of redemption is never, as in rational
and mystical religion, above the realm of living history,
but within and at the end of it. (p. 35)

There is, nevertheless, an eschatological element in,
and even basis for, the ethic of Jesus. The ethical demands made by Jesus are incapable of fulfillment in the
present existence of man. They proceed from a transcendent and divine unity of essential reality, and their final
fulfillment is possible only when God transmutes the
present chaos of this world into its final unity. . . . Plac-
ing the final fulfillment at the end of time and not in a
realm above temporality is to remain true to the genius
of prophetic religion and to state mythically what cannot
be stated rationally. (p. 59)

Niebuhr is entirely with us (or rather, was way ahead
of us) in seeing that moral activity is end-state oriented,
that its dynamic is the desire to move history from the
sinfulness of the present age toward God's future, the
kingdom, which is history's "essential reality." Niebuhr's is
—or starts out to be—ethics in a truly eschatological mode.
And when he moves on to describe the love ideal of the
kingdom, he again is found pointing toward what we have

described as eschatologically defined love. He supports what we have been saying; and if we may be so bold as to propose a seating protocol, we would put Niebuhr, Kierkegaard, the New Testament, and ourselves at one table representing a radical understanding of love—and the new morality at another, representing a much more wishy-washy position. Niebuhr, for instance, can say:

> The motive power of a love which transcends the impulses of nature ["the impulses of nature" would seem a rather apt characterization of the new morality's concept of love] is a combination of obedience to God and love of God [almost precisely what we have called "authorized" love]. (p. 190)
>
> The absolutism and perfectionism of Jesus' love ethic sets itself uncompromisingly not only against natural self-regarding impulses, but against the necessary prudent defenses of the self, required because of the egoism of others. . . . It has only a vertical dimension between the loving will of God and the will of man. (p. 45)
>
> . . . Emulation of the character of God is advanced as the only motive of forgiving enemies. Nothing is said about the possibility of transmuting their enmity to friendship through the practice of forgiveness. That social and prudential possibility has been read into the admonition of Jesus by liberal Christianity. . . . Every form of self-assertion is scrutinized and condemned in words which allow of no misinterpretation. (p. 46)
>
> [Jesus' ethic] is oriented by only one vertical religious reference, to the will of God; and the will of God is defined in terms of all-inclusive love. . . . Obedience to God, in the teachings of Jesus, must be absolute and must not be swayed by any ulterior considerations. (pp. 54–55)

Here are notes of rigor, commitment, demand, and discipline which are noticeably lacking within the new morality, but Niebuhr will not allow this reading of the New Testament to be compromised or toned down one little bit.

Over against this love perfectionism, however, Niebuhr brings in another theme, namely the conditions of sin under which human history transpires. Here again his position would seem to align very well with that of Kierkegaard, the New Testament, and—I hope—ourselves. Indeed, Kierkegaard and Niebuhr may be the two modern thinkers who have shown the liveliest sense of sin—both as to its economy in personal psychology and as a critique of social institutions and practices. And here again it is strikingly apparent that the new morality belongs at another table; its core admonition, "Go, love," makes sense only under the assumption that sin constitutes no serious obstacle in the following of that advice. Niebuhr speaks otherwise:

> The love commandment stands in juxtaposition to the fact of sin. It helps, in fact, to create the consciousness of sin. (p. 65)
>
> Prophetic religion attributes moral evil to an evil will rather than to the limitations of natural man. The justification for such an emphasis lies in the fact that human reason is actually able to envisage moral possibilities, more inclusive loyalties, and more adequate harmonies of impulse and life in every instance of moral choice than those which are actually chosen. There is, therefore, an element of perversity, a conscious choice of the lesser good, involved in practically every moral action; and certainly there are some actions in which this conscious perversity is the dominant force of action. (p. 75)

But, Niebuhr sees, sin shows itself not only as the inability to achieve love perfectionism but also as a tendency to misrepresent and scale down the ideal itself:

> Therefore the adjustment of modern religion to the "mind" of modern culture inevitably involved capitulation

to its thin "soul." . . . [Liberal Christianity's] Kingdom
of God was translated to mean exactly that ideal society
which modern culture hoped to realize through the evolu-
tionary process. Democracy and the League of Nations
were to be the political forms of this ideal. The Christian
ideal of love became the counsel of prudential mutuality
so dear and necessary to a complex commercial civiliza-
tion. The Christ of Christian orthodoxy, true mythical
symbol of both the possibilities and limits of the human,
became the good man of Galilee, symbol of human goodness and human possibilities without suggestion of the
limits of the human and the temporal—in short, without
the suggestion of transcendence. (p. 23)

Although the paragraph above—and so many more like
it in Niebuhr—is directed against an older liberalism, the
new morality is representative of a neoliberalism which is
challenged just as basically. The new moralists should
be required to give reason and cause why they need not
answer to Niebuhr.

To this point it is our feeling that Niebuhr and Kierkegaard would be in full agreement. It is as he proceeds to
his next step that Niebuhr's thought becomes distinctive
and marks a parting of the ways with Kierkegaard's.

Because human history transpires under the conditions
of sin, the achievement of love perfectionism is a manifest
impossibility. To attempt what clearly is impossible actually
is stupidity. Either one falsely assumes that what he has
achieved *is* the ideal—which is to pervert the ideal—or else
his efforts are irrelevant and even harmful because they fall
so far short of what he was attempting.

The all-out attempt to live according to Jesus' love perfectionism is irrelevant, but this is not to say that the
ideal itself is irrelevant. Indeed, the very title of Niebuhr's
crux chapter is "The Relevance of an Impossible Ethical
Ideal." He insists that the first requirement of an ethic is
that it be *realistic,* that it give signs of working, that there

be some evidence that the actions it advocates will bring beneficial results. Under the conditions of sin, then, this means that the ethic must support action which, first, is *practical* in a sinful society and, second, *possible* for a sinful agent. It is hard to argue with the good sense of this observation.

Nevertheless, realism dare not be the sole controlling principle of an ethic. In almost every case there is probably a higher action than the one we choose which, with a little imagination and daring, still could be found to be both practical and possible. The impossible ideal is relevant as it makes us guilty and discontent with our present choices and leads us to seek out higher possibilities:

> Yet this impossibility [of the ideal] is not one which can be relegated simply to the world of transcendence. It offers immediate possibilities of a higher good in every given situation. (p. 135)
>
> As the ideal of love must relate itself to the problems of a world in which its perfect realization is not possible, the most logical modification and application of the ideal in a world in which life is in conflict with life is the principle of equality which strives for an equilibrium in the conflict. (p. 136)

Niebuhr, with his ethic of realism, does not encourage one to shoot the moon (our analogy now assuming a pre-Apollo situation); you can't make it. Do shoot *toward* the moon; but be realistic in calculating how far your fuel and vehicle can take you, and don't try to go beyond that point. However, by keeping that dream moon always in view, you likely will discover that you can get higher than you thought you could.

Thus Niebuhr approves, encourages, and even asks that one scale down his immediate ethical goals from what Jesus' love perfectionism would require—*but this is not at all the same as scaling down the ideal itself* (he stoutly and consistently resists this move). The difference is crucial. If, say, Niebuhr's ethic brought one to a scaled-down action which coincided precisely with one sanctioned by the new morality, nevertheless the new morality would say, "Well done, good and faithful servant, you have expressed Christian love (and likely will invent a new way of doing so tomorrow); enter into the joy of your Lord," whereas Niebuhr would say, "Perhaps that was the best you could do at the moment, but it falls so far short of what Jesus taught that you had better ask God's forgiveness and see whether you can't find a way of doing better tomorrow." By maintaining a strong orientation toward Love's Authority, Niebuhr's ethic carries an incentive for commitment, effort, and heroism that the new morality largely lacks.

We have considerably more to say in regard to Niebuhr, but we want Kierkegaard in the picture when we do it. Let us turn our attention to his book *Works of Love*.

Kierkegaard's is simply a shoot-the-moon ethic. We will not take the time to trace out all his agreement with Niebuhr but merely elucidate the distinction. We shall try to contain ourselves; Kierkegaard says so much that we wish we had said and says it so well that we are tempted to quote page after page—and get our publisher all perturbed again.

The very first words of the book, Kierkegaard's invocatory prayer, pick up the crucial note which simply is not present in Niebuhr's presentation:

> How could anything rightly be said about love if Thou wert forgotten, Thou God of Love, from whom all love comes in heaven and on earth; Thou who didst hold nothing back but didst give everything in love; Thou who art love, so the lover is only what he is through being in Thee! (p. 4)[2]

---

[2] This and the following quotations from Kierkegaard's *Works of Love* are from the translation by David S. Swenson and Lillian M. Swenson (Copyright 1946, Princeton University Press). Reprinted by permission of Princeton University Press.

A few pages later, Kierkegaard makes the point even more strongly:

> As the peaceful lake is grounded deep in the hidden spring which no eye can see, so a man's love is grounded even deeper in the love of God. If there were at the bottom no wellspring, if God were not love, then there would be no quiet lake or human love. As the quiet lake is grounded darkly in the deep spring, so is human love mysteriously grounded in God's love. (p. 8)

For Niebuhr, God certainly is the definer of love, the authority in the sense of the one who prescribes the ideal; but he does not make it apparent that he appreciates the point made here by Kierkegaard and earlier by Browning, that God also is the mover and empowerer of Christian love, that the human lover actually becomes the agent through whom God does *his* loving.

Niebuhr hears two imperatives from God. Kierkegaard hears these but hears a third as well. Niebuhr hears "You *ought* to love" (the command of love perfectionism) and "You *cannot* love" (the recognition of our historical conditions of sin) and combines these to read "But you can and ought to be loving closer to the ideal than you are doing." Kierkegaard would not deny any of this, but the word which he hears above all others is Jesus' command, "Thou *shalt* love." The key section of Kierkegaard's book is an exposition of this phrase.

> Thus this "shalt" sets love free in blessed independence; such a love stands and falls not by some accidental circumstance of its object, it stands and falls by the law of eternity—but then it never falls; such a love does not depend upon this or that, it depends only on—the one liberating force, consequently it is eternally independent. (p. 33)
>
> When it [i.e., the eternal, which is Kierkegaard's rather

unfortunate code name for God] says, "Thou shalt love," then in saying that it says, "Thy love hath an everlasting validity." But it does not say this consolingly, for that would not help; it says it commandingly, just because there is something wrong. And when eternity says, "Thou shalt love," then it assumes the responsibility for guaranteeing that it can be done. (p. 35)

When both God and man are fully aware that man is nowhere near capable of practicing love perfectionism and God nevertheless commands "Thou *shalt* love," this is as much as a promise that, if man will try, God will see to the success of the effort. Kierkegaard drives the point even deeper in a later exposition:

The God-relationship is the sign by which the love for men is recognized as genuine. As soon as the love-relationship does not lead me to God, and as soon as I in the love-relationship do not lead the other man to God, then is the love, even if it is the greatest happiness and delight of affection, even if to the lovers it is the highest good of the earthly life, still not the true love. The world can never get this into its head, that God does not thus merely become the third party in every love-relation, but really becomes the sole object of affection, so it is not the husband who is the wife's beloved, but it is God; and it is the wife who is helped by her husband to love God, and conversely, and so on. The merely human interpretation of love can never get any further than reciprocity: the lover is the beloved, and the beloved is the lover. Christianity teaches that such a love has not yet found its right object—God. A love-relationship is threefold: the lover, the beloved, the love; but the love is God. And, therefore, to love another man is to help him to love God, and to be loved is to be helped to love God. (pp. 98–99)

An analogy, perhaps, can help elucidate his point. Natural man sees the relationship thus: The lover is a light bulb that generates the candle power that shines directly upon its object, the beloved. Kierkegaard has a much more sophisticated setup: God is the light source whose energy is directed by the mirror which is the human lover. But God (in particular his law and teaching, which we shall investigate in the next chapter) is involved again as the lens which focuses the light so as to shine upon the beloved. God plays a role which goes far beyond that envisioned even by Niebuhr.

And Kierkegaard saw that this understanding involves an eschatological perspective—and that statement forces me into a confession. Before I started writing this exposition of *Works of Love* it had been a couple of years since I had read the book. In the interim my thought had turned explicitly to the theology of hope. I suspected that Kierkegaard's thought was much more eschatologically oriented than ever had been recognized, had expressed that opinion in print a couple times, and even had begun to collect evidence with a view to making the case. Then, in the *Christian Century* article that now forms the first chapter of this book, I had moved toward applying the theology of hope to the matter of ethics. Finally, under Doubleday's prodding for this book, I came to explore the possibility that the New Testament understanding of *love* is itself eschatologically oriented. And now I discover that Kierkegaard had said all this in so many words (not quite "in so many words"; he failed to use the approved vocabulary of today's theology of hope and so has prevented his contribution from being discovered). But this is the story of my life: All of my most original ideas were thought up by Søren Kierkegaard—although I do deserve credit for my choice of *whom* I was going to second-guess.

To start with, here is as penetrating an insight into the theology of hope as has been made:

This is the turning point in world-history. Christianity the religion of the *future*. Paganism was the religion of the present or of the past (pre-existence). Even Judaism was too present-minded in spite of its prophetic character; it was a futurity in the present; Christianity is a present *in futuro*.[3]

That last I take to mean that Judaism extrapolates the future out of the reality of the present, while Christianity introduces the reality of the future *into* the present. "The truest thing that can be said about the present is that it is God's future in process of becoming," as I have been putting it.

However, Kierkegaard's more detailed presentation of his theology of hope is the section in which he expounds upon Paul's phrase "Love hopes all things." Again we must call attention to the code words which Kierkegaard uses in place of such terms as "eschatology," "the kingdom of God," et al. "The eternal" denotes God and—perhaps even more precisely put—God in his kingly ruling. "The good," on the other hand, denotes the order of things that God's kingly rule brings into being. Kierkegaard's two words cover the two ideas which scholars discover in the biblical usage "kingdom of God." Kierkegaard nowhere defines his terms in this way (nor in any other way) but the meanings fit—and are the only ones that will fit in this and many other passages from Kierkegaard's work.

Hoping lays hold upon the future, on the possibility, which again, as distinguished from reality, is always a duality—the possibility of progress or retrogression, of building up or tearing down, of good or of evil. The eternal *"is,"* but when the eternal touches on the temporal, or is in the temporal, they do not meet each other in

[3] *Papirer* VIII[1]A305. This journal entry is quoted as a footnote by the translators, Howard and Edna Hong, in their edition of *Works of Love* (New York: Harper Torchbooks, 1964), p. 371, n. 14.

the "present," for then the present would itself be the
eternal. . . . Hence when the eternal is in the temporal,
then it is in the future (for the present cannot lay hold
on it, and the past is past) or in the possibility. The
past is the actual, the future the possible; the eternal is
everlastingly the eternal; in time the eternal is the possible, the future. . . . If a man who is concerned with
the possible lays hold equally on the duality of the possible, then we say: he is *expectant*. Expecting contains in
itself the same duality as does the possible, and to expect
is to relate oneself to the possible clearly and only as such.
On that the relationship divides, inasmuch as the expectant man makes a choice. To lay hold expectantly on
the possibility of the good is *to hope,* which just for this
reason cannot be any temporal expectation, but is an
eternal hope. To lay hold expectantly on the possibility of
evil is *to fear.* . . . Yet as soon as the choice is made,
the possible is changed, for the possibility of the good is
the eternal. . . . By the decision to choose hope one de-
cides, therefore, infinitely more than it seems, for it is
an eternal decision. . . . In the making of a distinction
(and choice is the making of a distinction) is the possibility of the good more than possibility, for it is the
eternal. Hence it happens that he who hopes can never
be deceived; for to hope is to expect the possibility of
the good, but the possibility of the good is the eternal.
(pp. 201–2)

Whoever stakes his life upon the fact and lives as though
the future is to bring the kingly rule of God is not simply
choosing one option out of several; he has chosen *the*
option and in that choice opened the way for God to
introduce his kingly rule. Because God works as an actual,
end-seeking power in history, to "hope" is to *enable* the
coming of the very end for which one hopes. And Kierkegaard sees that this sort of hope is practically synonymous
with love:

So it is with hoping all things. But *lovingly* to hope everything indicates the relation of the lover to other men, so that in his relation to them, in hoping for them, he always keeps the door of possibility open with infinite preference for the possibility of the good. Hence, he lovingly hopes that at every moment there is the possibility, the possibility of the good for the other man; this, the possibility of the good, indicates the increasingly glorious progress in the good from perfection unto perfection, or the rising again after the fall, or salvation from perdition, and so on. (p. 205)

No one can hope unless he also is loving; he cannot *hope for himself* without also being loving, for the good qualities hang infinitely together; but if he is loving, he also has hope for others. . . . The true lover says: "Hope everything, give up no man, for to give him up is to give up your love for him—for if you do not give that up, then you have hope. But if you give up your love for him, then you cease to be the lover." (p. 206)

If there were no love, then neither would there be hope; it would be like a letter which lies uncalled for. If there were no love, it would be with hope as with a letter whose contents would be so very welcome, but where there was no one to deliver the letter. Then love, although greater than hope, would assume it as its duty and its task, to bring hope. (p. 209)

So consistent is the Scripture usage, it does not call all kinds of expectation, the expectation of the manifold, hope; it knows only one hope, *the hope,* the possibility of the good and . . . having it, say the Scriptures, is an honor which shall not be put to shame. (p. 212)

Later in his book, after Kierkegaard has moved to an exposition of "Love Abideth," he retains the eschatological orientation of love:

Oh, and to this belong the powers of eternity, in the decisive moment, immediately to transform the past into

the future! Yet it has this power of abiding. . . . So
with the lover. That it came to a breach cannot be plainly
seen, it can only be known by an understanding of the
past. But the lover will not know the past, for he abides;
and abiding is in the direction of the future. Hence the
lover expresses the fact that the relationship, which the
other calls a breach, is a relationship which is not yet finished. . . . But the lover who abides constantly extricates
himself from his knowledge of the past; he knows no past,
he waits only on the future. (pp. 247–48)

This is enough to give the gist of Kierkegaard's thought,
but we dare not leave *Works of Love* without sharing what
can pass for his judgment on the new morality:

The Christian doctrine is frequently presented as a certain soft, almost enervated form of love. After all, there
is love and love; you predict for yourself and for your
own flesh and blood, good days or happy days without
anxiety, for God is love and love—about austerity there
must be nothing said; everything must be about the free
and easy language and nature of love. Yet thus understood, God's love easily becomes a fabulous and childish
conception, the figure of Christ something so insipid and
mawkish as to render it impossible that He could have
been a stumbling block to the Jews or foolishness to the
Greeks: that is, as Christianity was taught in our child-
hood. (p. 303)

You've got to be good to fire a salvo like that more than a
century before the target hove into view.

Reinhold Niebuhr, although well aware of the New Testament's love perfectionism, in the interests of "realism" is
willing to scale down ethical demand to where it is prac-
ticable under the conditions of sin. Søren Kierkegaard,
fully aware of the conditions of sin, does not so much as

hint that a scaling down is proper under any circumstances. What option is there except to declare one man right and the other wrong?

Although he does not face up to the fact, Niebuhr actually has implied a rather serious charge against the New Testament. He would have to admit, I think, that he has no scriptural support in his deliberately posting of counsels for action *below* the demands of the absolutist love ethic. Is it because the biblical writers—as the liberals Niebuhr castigates—are naïve in overlooking the presence and significance of sin? Obviously not; it was from this same New Testament that Niebuhr derived his own understanding of sin. Or can it be that the Scripture teaches too low a view of love? Niebuhr would have a hard time explaining why the New Testament writers did not feel impelled to make the same adjustment he feels impelled to make.

On the other hand, according to his lights, Niebuhr would have to judge the ethic of Kierkegaard and the New Testament as reckless: It fails to reckon with human finiteness and sin. Yet is it not actually the case that Kierkegaard recks with more rather than with less than Niebuhr does? Niebuhr has failed to reckon with the fact that God is actively present and available, forwarding his kingly rule and bringing it to consummation, and that this has the effect of opening possibilities which simply are not calculable by sinful man as being options under history's conditions of sin. He fails to reckon that, through a Pippa who strives only to obey implicitly the demands of love perfectionism, more could be accomplished than any calculation would have believed possible. A Kierkegaard can afford to act in a way that the world would call *reckless,* because he has reckoned on the promise of the kingdom and the God who even now is busy at that promise.

Although Niebuhr used more explicitly eschatological language than Kierkegaard did, in the final analysis his eschatology proves to be less than realistic. He says:

The apocalypse is a mythical expression of the impossible possibility under which all human life stands. The Kingdom of God is always at hand in the sense that impossibilities are really possible, and lead to new actualities in given moments of history. Nevertheless every actuality of history reveals itself, after the event, as only an approximation of the ideal; and the Kingdom of God is therefore not here. It is in fact always coming but never here. (p. 60)

Niebuhr cannot be faulted for his phrase "mythical expression," if by that he means that the biblical accounts of the kingdom are not necessarily to be understood as literal description of the end state of history. But when he says that the kingdom is *"never* here," one suspects that his intention about myth goes even deeper. The kingdom, now, is one with his impossible ideal; it has no real existence in the present nor is it an actual possibility for the future; it is a shining ideal, a carrot on a stick (never accessible and, in this case, not even a real carrot), designed to entice man ever forward. And it must be said that, in Niebuhr's ethic, God himself plays only this same sort of role. God sets the definition of love, and love is motivated as obedience to him; God calls forth man's best moral possibilities; but there is no suggestion that God can lift men beyond themselves, that he can work within them that which creates incalculable, more-than-human possibilities. The idea of God draws men to higher accomplishment within the sinful conditions of history, but there is not the real power of a God who is creating new men and a consummated history.

Kierkegaard's shoot-the-moon ethic, on the other hand, is built on the paradigm of Christ's passion. "Having loved his own who were in the world, he loved them to the end" (John 13:1). When it became obvious that that end was to be the cross, it must have seemed that the love should cease or take some other tack—call down angels from heaven, let his servants fight, disappear, anything. There was no possible human calculation that could project going to the cross as being realistic, relevant, prudential, or practical either for Jesus or his cause. There was no conceivable way in which this action could be made to spell victory. So, without the assurance of calculation—indeed, in utter defiance of calculation—Jesus went ahead and obeyed God in the sheer love-hope of which Kierkegaard speaks. The calculation proved correct; Jesus died and his cause was defeated, but then . . . (*"Now,* Frodo!") EUCA-TASTROPHE (You thought we had forgotten that word, didn't you?): *God raised him from the dead.*

When our God of Love is determined to bring in his kingdom, he can use man's obedience in upsetting the very surest of human calculations—even if it requires a resurrection from the dead to do it! If, then, it is this God with whom we deal and the promise of his kingdom upon which we act, how dare we limit our obedience to what *we* can calculate as being practical!

Obviously, for our part we have chosen Søren Kierkegaard over Reinhold Niebuhr as teacher of the truly Christian ethic of love perfectionism, the ethic of promise— *but this does not mean that we have rejected Niebuhr or his ethic.* Recall that he spoke much about "social problems" and about how society as such should meet these problems. He apparently was thinking about an ethic for man in the mass.

But, among men in the mass (among even church members, to say nothing of secular political groupings), how many are there who have heard this promise of the kingdom and have sufficient confidence in it that they would choose obedience to love perfectionism when all calculations would call it folly? How many men are willing to stake their lives on the possibility of a eucatastrophe? Obviously the ethic of promise will never win more than a small minority, will not find anything like mass acceptance; it is too rigorous and daring.

Has, then, Christian ethics nothing to say to the mass of men, nothing to say in the arena where society wrestles with its social problems? Here, I submit, is where Reinhold Niebuhr can and should be heard. Our chapter heading, with its reference to a double moral standard, carries a serious intention. Kierkegaard's (and our ethic of promise) is a Christian ethic directed to Christians, heart-and-soul Christians. Niebuhr's is a Christian ethic addressed to nominal Christians and non-Christians. (And as regards those who cannot accept even the tension and demand of his impossible ideal, I suppose we should hope that they will follow at least the new morality.)

Granted, this talk about a double moral standard creates problems, but the alternatives are worse. If Christianity were to insist simply on its own ethical norm, all or nothing, it would leave government, civil institutions, and society as a whole without influence or guidance. If, on the other hand, out of concern for the world it were to scale down its ethical norm to what is relevant to the world, it would betray its Lord, hamper the coming of the kingdom, and lose the possibility of performing its ultimate service to the world. Christianity must play it both ways at once: requiring the one standard of its own and those who desire to be recognized as such; teaching the second standard to those who are ready to accept only that much; never allowing the one ethic to displace the other.

The pinch will be felt by the Christian who is called upon to live in both worlds—caught up in the overlap (to hark back to our earlier discussion). As a Christian and a member of a Christian community (i.e., his church congregation—if even it qualifies; we deny that civil, political communities can in any sense be called Christian) he strives to live out of one ethic; as a citizen he must be involved in groups where those standards will not even be recognized, let alone demanded.

Although, of course, Niebuhr would not agree with the way in which we have divided the field between his love perfection ethic and his realistic one, he does see very clearly the danger that comes in trying to mix the two:

> The principal defect of the liberal Christian thought on the question of violence is that it confuses two perspectives upon the problem, the pragmatic and the perfectionist one. Both have their legitimacy. But moral confusion results from the efforts to compound them. . . . Realism is lacking in every modern religious idealism which thinks it possible to be involved in all the moral relativities, incident upon the defense of limited human groups, beginning with the family and ending with the nation, and yet be true to an absolute ethic by the simple expedient of disavowing violence. . . . A responsible relationship to the political order, therefore, makes an unqualified disavowal of violence impossible. (pp. 167–70)

Niebuhr here puts his finger upon the nub of the dilemma. How does the Christian who is living out of one set of assumptions relate to and operate within a society that takes for granted a radically different set of assumptions? Let us keep the discussion within our context rather than Niebuhr's (i.e., assume that a God of eucatastrophic capabilities makes perfectionism much more relevant than he would grant) yet follow up his thought, retaining his case study of violence and military violence in particular—even though much of what we say will have application to other moral issues as well.

Let us use different sorts of ball games as an analogy. Now, advancing the ball by *running* it represents the sort of violence in which, under our assumption, Christians cannot conscientiously engage. By this token the Christian would have no difficulty in playing *basketball*—where running with the ball is outlawed by the very rules of the game. Obviously, however, in this world the name of the international relations game is *football*, not basketball. So-ciety takes it as axiomatic that military preparations and actions are within the rules and, under the proper circum-stances, are both ethical and necessary. So the world insists that the game is *football*; the Christian insists that it must be *basketball*. But the situation does not stay that simple.

Remember that the rules of football do not specify that the ball can be advanced *only* by running it; passing also is a live and viable option. And of course, even under the present rules violence is not the *only* recognized mode of international relations, the ball can be advanced in many non-violent ways. This consideration opens several different positions regarding non-violence—positions which actually have very little in common with one another: (1) A person can insist that only basketball is the truly Christian game and refuse to participate in football. (2) However, even a person who has no qualms against playing football, who fully accepts the game and its rules, very validly may feel that the game would go better *as a football game* if the team were to try more passes and fewer runs. The question here is simply one of football strategy, not of whether it is the proper game. (3) One could maintain that football games can be played and won using only pass plays, without running the ball at all. This is the position that Niebuhr identifies as "liberal" and, with considerable justice in our opinion, brands as muddleheaded.

Position 3 is a mishmash of 1 and 2. Its argument regarding strategy winds up demanding a radical change in the rules: The best way to play *football* is to follow the rules of *basketball!* What kind of a game is that? It should be apparent that football minus running plays does not equal basketball. Under our assumption, basket-ball (the complete renunciation of violence) is premised upon faith in a God who can redeem a situation which from a human standpoint should eventuate only in disaster. The proposal that, divine intervention quite aside, human non-violent love will "work" as the practical mode of worldly politics is indeed a galimatias that belongs neither to basketball nor to football.

Given, then, this football-basketball frame of reference, what are proper Christian actions and what are not?

It would seem entirely proper for the Christian to refuse to join the football team; this is what conscientious objection means. It would be proper for him to argue loud and long (although also rationally and lovingly) with his compatriots that football is all wrong, a bad game. What would seem to be improper would be that, once the group decision has been made that football is the name of the game, the Christian take his place in the backfield and then refuse to carry the ball when it comes to him, or to take his place in the line and then refuse to block for one who is carrying the ball. Likewise, he is guilty of the very violence he deplores if he tries to break up or undercut the game the group has decided to play—*persuade* them to play another game, yes, but not *subvert* the one they are playing. Niebuhr is right; one ought either to stay out of the game entirely or, if he chooses to become a player, be willing to play by the rules that are in effect.

There is another proper Christian action which is of a different order than those we have mentioned. The Christian might honestly and rightfully counsel that the football game would go better if the team would do less running of the ball and more passing. But he must be very careful at this point that his counsel actually is in the interests of the football game and not a reflection of his personal disapproval of football as such; he has no right to introduce into the game actions which are based upon premises foreign to the game itself.

Here is raised the problem of which the historic peace churches once were keenly aware but which has been ignored almost entirely by the modern pacifist movement, namely, can a Christian hold office in government? To what extent does he thus become a member of the football team? The issue is not—as commonly has been assumed—that nice Christians do not dirty their hands in politics. It is: Can it be fair to society for a Christian to take a position of power and influence and, in the name of and on behalf of the group, take actions that proceed out of premises that the group does not buy? Has he a right to commit society to a position it would in nowise accept, jeopardize the ball game it has chosen to play, or make it play a ball game it has no desire to play? It is true that our coins are inscribed "In God We Trust," but it should be obvious that neither the United States nor any other country is about to the place that it defenselessly will risk national martyrdom on the strength of a promise that the God who resurrected Jesus Christ also is capable of resurrecting a nation in the course of establishing his kingdom. Christians and Christian communities are called upon to take that risk; secular institutions cannot be expected to. However, Christians do have a right to challenge society to a *Niebuhrian* ethic, i.e., to find the most loving possibilities that still can be calculated as prudential under the world's premises.

But Niebuhr would seem to be on solid ground in his scorn for the naïveté of the "liberals" who would contend that absolute love perfectionism is prudential under the terms of worldly calculation; who would contend that *human* love, the love of sinful agents unassisted by the intervention of a God of eucatastrophic capabilities, is a practical and possible solution to the human dilemma; who would contend that a *football* game can be won without running the ball.

This point raises some interesting considerations. With whom does the defenseless, God-hoping Christian have the most in common: with the "liberal" who shares his commitment to love perfectionism but without the supportive commitment to the enabling promise of the kingdom, or with the secularist who agrees that love perfectionism is not practical (unless there is enablement from God)?

To what extent can the defenseless, God-hoping Christian

join forces with those who are selling and even attempting
to force through a love perfectionism on a basis that the
Christian himself considers completely inadequate and un-
workable?

Does there not open a rather yawning gulf between the
conscientious objection of Christian absolutists—those who
stake their position on the uncalculable possibilities opened
by a kingdom-creating God—and that of all prudential
pacifists? This latter group necessarily includes all *selective*
objectors who demur only at particular wars; obviously, if
the capability of God is the justification of defenselessness,
God is as capable of handling Hitler (the war that usually
is defended as justifiable) as of handling Vietnam (the war
that often is condemned as unjustifiable). The distinction
between just and unjust wars can exist only in terms of a
prudential ethic.

Consider that Christian absolutism brings into the ethical
calculus a totally new factor, the possibility of God's intervention, which the non-pacifist does not recognize. On
the contrary, prudential pacifism (whether absolutist or
selective) is a position based on precisely the same set of
factors that the non-pacifist is using. The difference is simply
a matter of opinion as to whether a run or a pass will
best forward the game at the moment. Is it proper that
a man not simply argue with the team but even attempt
to break up the game, because he feels that there has been
chosen a poor series of plays? (I mean that as an open
and not a rhetorical question; my point is simply that
the conscientious objection of Christian absolutism and of
prudential pacifism are horses of two vastly different colors,
bred out of two vastly different ethics, needing to be ap-
proached in vastly different ways and judged according to
vastly different norms.)

Finally, this double moral standard—one standard of
which the Christian requires of himself and his community
but which he would not think of requiring of the world,
the other of which he requires of the world but which

would be a betrayal of his faith for him to adopt for
himself—forces us to take a new look at the position
which for a long time was espoused by the historic peace
churches but which more recently even they have tended to
brand as hypocritical. Although it sounds two-faced, is
there not a true consistency in the following position: As a
Christian, John Doe cannot support or participate in the
Vietnam war; he understands the New Testament love
ethic as prohibiting such. He wishes that society at large
saw the matter so and banks upon the power of God to
take care of things if any nation or group of nations became
willing to choose defenseless love obedience. He is *not*
glad that other men are fighting to defend him; he would
rather they did not. *If the nation were Christian,* his counsel would be that it withdraw from Vietnam without consideration of consequences, dissolve its armed forces, and
give up so much as the thought of ever engaging in warfare
again. But such action becomes even a possibility only upon
the premise of a quality of hope that the world cannot
now accept. John Doe's counsel to the world, therefore, is
different than that which he would speak to his fellow
Christians or be willing to follow for himself, namely,
"Listen to Reinhold Niebuhr and seek the most loving way
possible within the limits of prudential human calculation."
That might be a gradual, supervised withdrawal from South
Vietnam; it might be (at least the possibility cannot be
categorically excluded) the atom bombing of Hanoi.

It should be clear that what we are talking about has
little if anything in common with Luther's doctrine of the
two realms and such suggestions. Luther's thought is that
the Christian is governed by, must live out of, two different
ethics—one in his personal deportment and in the church,
the other in his life as a citizen and member of society
at large. What we are saying, rather, is that the Christian
should strive to live solely and entirely from the absolute
ethic of Christian love, but that he recognize that it
would be irrelevant and futile to expect or even counsel

non-Christian society to take the same sort of risks that he is willing to take for himself. The person who has heard the promise of the kingdom and trusts in the God who can bring that kingdom to pass even if it takes such incalculable prodigies as exoduses of slaves, destructions of holy cities ("I will make the valley of Achor [Trouble] a door of hope" [Hosea 2:15]), returns from exiles, resurrections from the dead, comings in power by Holy Spirits, and who knows what more yet to happen—this person can afford to do some high-risk loving that no sane man (read, non-believer) would attempt (nor would it be fair to ask him to attempt it).

"My kingship is not of this world; *if* my kingship were of this world, my servants *would* fight, that I might not be handed over to the Jews; but my kingship is not from the world" (John 18:36).

Of course the Christian is out to help as many others as possible become Christian, to help them hear the promise of the kingdom; and he lives for the day when the entire world shall be brought to that place. For himself and for his Christian brethren he has no intention of scaling down the love demand in any regard, in any sphere of life and activity; but until such time as the world has the wherewithal for heroism, he is willing to help that world find the most loving actions possible *under its premises,* although they may be actions that he never would approve for himself. But what we resist is the implication of the new morality and many other modern moralities, namely, that Christians and non-Christians are little enough different that one can find between them some sort of compromise ethic to which both can aspire and which can be expected of both—perhaps expecting the Christians to do a little better in living up to it (yet perhaps expecting the very reverse; the new morality contains considerable glorification of the liberated, secular man). But if we may put the matter bluntly: That isn't the way the New Testament has it!

So although we recognize the need and justification of

Christian ethical guidance for the non-Christian world
(better, for "the world" which in fact is non-Christian),
our ethic of promise is rather the attempt to find the first-
order Christian ethic for Christians and Christian communities. Our concern in the earlier chapters and in those following is with this one particular ethic.

7

There Ought to Be a Law

———◆◆◆———

The new morality, we suggested in an earlier chapter, can be understood in large part as a revolt against authoritarianism. In that respect it also is a revolt against law, for law and authoritarianism are thought of as two sides of the same coin. But just as we saw that there is authoritarianism and there is authority, we need to see that there is law and there is law. The new morality wants to go with the one law of love—although as vaguely as love is defined it is a question in how far even this can be called "a law." But even while recognizing a certain justification in the revolt, we plead for a closer look at what law can be and should be, how it can be a support rather than a threat to love.

The book which develops the concept of Christian love, namely the Bible, also develops a concept of law to go along with it—both sponsored by the same God. What we think of as "law" is only one type of law—better, one perversion of law. Almost invariably we think of law in *prescriptive* terms. The law *prescribes* what one must do in order to be saved, to be accepted, to be okayed. "Do this and this and this and this, and then God will let you in."

But truth to tell, the biblical idea of "salvation" (or "redemption") isn't even what we have in mind when we think this way. "Salvation," to our minds, is a state of secure accomplishment, a having arrived, a getting it made, a coming home free; it is in effect to have achieved an end state. But this is not biblical eschatology, for it makes the end state a present or even past *achievement* rather than a future *desideratum*. The Bible sees salvation otherwise.

Rather clearly, throughout the Old Testament and to a considerable extent in the New, the paradigm of salvatory event is Passover, Israel's escape from Egypt. The Book of Exodus devotes a disproportionate amount of space to this part of the biblical story. The language used is of the most exalted sort:

> It was a night of watching by the Lord to bring them out of the land of Egypt; so this same night is a night of watching kept to the Lord by all the people of Israel throughout their generations. (Exodus 12:42) . . . Remember this day, in which you came out from Egypt, out of the house of bondage, for by strength of hand the Lord brought you out from this place. . . . And you shall tell your son on that day, "It is because of what the Lord did for me when I came out of Egypt." And it shall be to you as a sign on your hand and as a memorial between your eyes, that the law of the Lord may be in your mouth; for with a strong hand the Lord has brought you out of Egypt. (Exodus 13:3–9)

The Passover festival has become the central commemoration of Judaism unto the present day; and the Lord's Supper, the central commemoration of Christianity, essentially is a new Passover. Perhaps most striking of all is the fact that the arrival in the Promised Land—which might seem to be a more appropriate symbol of salvation— has never posed any threat to Passover at all. No, the escape from Egypt is *the* biblical picture of salvation.

Yet a week or two after the event, in the wilderness

of Sinai, approach one of these come-out Israelites and put it to him, "Brother, are you saved?"

"You trying to kid me or something? If *this* is salvation, I'll take the fleshpots of unsaved Egypt just any old day!"

And yet that man's children and his children's children to a hundred generations have proclaimed that he *was* saved, he was indeed saved.

In what, then, does salvation consist? Obviously not in having *arrived* anywhere. Let us suggest three elements. First, it consists in being freed, in being loosed from restraint so that one can set his own direction, form a new grouping, gather into a new community, become a separate people. Most of all, one is made free to travel. In the second place, salvation consists in finding—or being found by—a leader-lord, one who shows the way and indeed *makes* the way. This, in biblical terms, is what a "savior" is, a leader-lord rather than one who *plucks* passive brands from the burning. In the third place, salvation consists in being set upon and being enabled to go upon the way that the leader-lord is making through the world to his kingdom. Salvation describes the beginning of a way rather than its end, speaks of a promise in process rather than an accomplishment secured.

There is abundant evidence that the New Testament understands salvation in the same way. At several points the Savior Jesus is likened to the old leader-lord Moses. The most impressive instance is in Stephen's defense before the Sanhedrin. Stephen traces the biblical history up to the point where God sends Moses to the Israelite slaves in Egypt and then says:

> This Moses whom they refused, saying, "Who made you a ruler and a judge?" God sent as both ruler and deliverer by the hand of the angel that appeared to him in the bush. He led them out, having performed wonders and signs in Egypt and at the Red Sea and in the wilderness for forty years. This is the Moses who said

to the Israelites, "God will raise up for you a prophet
from your brethren as he raised me up."

(Acts 7:35–37)

Clearly, the intent is to draw the parallel between the leader-
lord of the old exodus and that of the new.

In the Gospel of John, Jesus at times speaks in the
role of a new Moses; the third chapter of Hebrews makes
an explicit comparison of the two; and in an interesting
touch, Revelation 15:3 reports of the saints around the
heavenly throne, "And they sing the song of Moses, the
servant of God, and the song of the Lamb"—and there
follows just one song.

The concept of "savior" is carried over from the Old
Testament to the New, and there are plenty of indicators
that the concept of salvation comes over similarly. The
most striking documentation is perhaps the hymn that Luke
attributes to Zechariah at the birth of John the Baptist:

Blessed be the Lord God of Israel,
for he has visited and redeemed his people,
and has raised up a horn of salvation for us . . .
that we should be saved from our enemies, . . .
to perform the mercy promised to our fathers,
and to remember his holy covenant,
. . . to grant us
that we, being delivered from the hand of our enemies,
might serve him without fear,
in holiness and righteousness before him all the
    days of our life. . . .
For you will go before the Lord to prepare his ways,
to give knowledge of salvation to his people . . .
to give light to those who sit in darkness and in
    the shadow of death.
to guide our feet into the way of peace.

(Luke 1:68–79)

All of the elements of salvation which we developed out of the exodus model recur here. So if we think of law as being the prescription of what one must do to *attain* "salvation," we have slipped off the biblical concept of salvation (which is not an "attainment") to say nothing of law; the concept of law is governed by the concept of salvation.

But coming to look at law itself, it is doubtful even whether our English word "law," with all its prescriptive overtones, is the best translation for what the Bible is talking about. The Hebrew word is *torah,* and it would be closer to the mark to think of it as teaching, counsel, instruction, guidance. In the Old Testament tradition it is clear the *torah* was not experienced as restriction, coercion, authoritarianism. Quite the contrary, it was welcomed as God's greatest gift to man, valued as a manifestation of his willingness to help his people find the style of everyday life that would be most satisfying and productive for them.

This law was *descriptive* rather than *prescriptive* in character. Rather than telling people what they *must* do to be saved, it was a description of what they *can* do and what they will *want* to do now that they *are* saved. The *torah* is a *description* of the life-style of an Israelite who through God's mighty acts has been put upon the way of salvation, is God's helpful suggestions as to how a grateful Israelite can proceed to show his gratitude by living out the salvation he has been given. There is evidence that, in the world out of which the Ten Commandments came, law in general tended to be viewed from much more of a descriptive perspective than is the case today; and the very structure of the Ten Commandments gives support to this judgment.

In fact, the Ten Commandments will provide us a very good test case, because, with their negative wording, they represent precisely the sort of thing that the new morality is most hot against. What modern liberated man just will not abide is to have someone telling him, "No, no, no, remember the sabbath, honor father and mother, no, no, no, no, no!" (Some scholars believe that even four and five originally were worded in the negative.)

But originally the Ten Commandments were neither spoken nor heard that way. For one thing, their negative wording actually is a guarantee of freedom. That's a fact; a negative command prohibits one limited type of activity but leaves a person free to choose between a myriad others. For example, "Thou shalt not eat spinach," a negative command, grants a person very wide latitude indeed in choosing what to eat. On the other hand, a positively stated command, "Thou shalt eat spinach once a day," would be a terribly oppressive edict, if not completely impossible in some parts of the world, during certain seasons, at many times in history. The "negativity" of the Ten Commandments has nothing to do with whether or not they are restrictive and freedom-denying.

But more to the point, the Ten Commandments are put together in such a way as to deny the prescriptive and cry for the descriptive mode of interpretation. We read amiss whenever we read the Commandments by starting with Exodus 20:3 and Commandment 1. Verse 2, the prologue, is essential to all that follows. It reads: "I am the Lord your God, who brought you out of the land of Egypt, out of the house of bondage." Rather plainly put: "You are saved men! I did it for you without making any demands, setting any prerequisites, or even asking into the state of your piety. I saved you because that is what I decided I wanted to do. Now, being saved, I assume that you would welcome and could use a brief description of what a saved Israelite looks like. Glad to help; in the first place, he will have no other gods before me," etc.

In context (and we value that blessed state as much as any contextualist does) the Ten Commandments definitely do not say: "All right, you damned [i.e., unsaved] Israelites, here it is: one, two, three, four, five, six, seven, eight, nine, ten. Go see what you can do with those. When you think you've got them made, come back, and I'll see whether or not you're fit for my salvation. World without end. Amen."

At least here in its pristine purity, "law" meant something quite different from, something much more beautiful and loving than that which the new morality now is rebelling against. But sad to say, this understanding did not last. Particularly in the period following the Babylonian Exile, Judaism tended to go legalistic, perverting the *torah* from description into a most detailed and exacting prescription—and so the Pharisees with whom Jesus had something of a run-in.

It can be argued, even, that that go-around represents nothing so much as Jesus' attempt to restore the *torah* to its original mode. Of course, he was *called* a destroyer of the law, but in actuality he was closer to the truth of the law than were the professionals who supposedly were defending it. The New Testament scholar Johannes Munck has spoken directly to our point:

> The difference consisted, not in [Jesus'] neglecting to observe the whole of the Jewish rules and commandments, but in his view of God's will, and therefore his interpretation of the Law, both of which were different from those common to the Jews. For him God's requirements were much stricter than the Law and the Jewish interpretations; but God's love was much stronger than the Jews had realized.[1]

We have some interesting juxtapositions here. The observation about seeing God's requirements as stricter is only partly true; in matters of ritual and churchly nitpickery (sabbath observance, dietary regulations, mint and dill and cummin) Jesus' thrust clearly was to relax—if not abolish—the law. However, as regards morality—the

[1] *Paul and the Salvation of Mankind* (Richmond, Va.: John Knox Press, 1959), p. 271.

"weightier matters" that are here our particular interest—
it is very true that his reading is much stricter ("every one
who *looks* at a woman lustfully," "every one who is angry,"
"do not resist one who is evil," "it has been said, but I
say").

Yet he introduced this strictness in the very process of
fighting legalism, of making the law less burdensome and
oppressive. Clearly, the only way such a two-way switch
could be accomplished is, as Munck hints, by changing the
very concept "law" in the process—which change, in our
terminology, was a move from prescription to description.
Prescriptive law is law seen as an end in itself; God is far
away, and the law is set up in his place. One's immediate
relationships are directed to and focused upon the statutes;
and if (*if*) one makes it with them, then God might be
willing to grant him audience. Descriptive law, on the other
hand, brings God close and then steps aside (not, disappears) so that God and man can talk; in fact, the law *is*
this talk.

Now the closer a man gets to God—the *holy* God—
the more directly he hears his will and the stricter the requirement becomes. It is inevitable; the padding between,
the intermediary muffling and dispersion, has been removed. And yet when God comes closer, the law, although
more strict, becomes less burdensome. This too is inevitable,
because, in the first place, the relationship now is one of
personal counsel rather than impersonal edict, and in the
second place, as Munck points out, the coming close of
God makes his love—his *enabling* love—stronger to an
even greater degree than it makes his requirement stricter.

If the Ten Commandments were our model of descriptive law in its pristine purity, the Sermon on the Mount is
its model in the perfection of redemption. The evidence is
that the Matthew author intentionally presents the Sermon
as being the new *torah;* and it, although stricter than the
old, is even more tellingly descriptive in form and character.

For one thing, the speaker is Jesus and the hearers are,

in the original setting, his *disciples* and, since that time, the church which is his *body*. This may seem to be a pointing out of the obvious; but if these teachings are treated as though it were a matter of indifference as to who originated them, or if they are taken as addressed to anybody and everybody indiscriminately, the significance of the Sermon is jeopardized. The relationship within which the teaching takes place is every bit as important as the content of the teaching itself; one must have heard the promise before he has any inclination to hear the demand. When Moses was the deliverer of the law it took a sentence to specify that the commandments were not his but those of the Savior Yahweh who already has "brought you out." The Sermon makes the same point but does not require a written verse to do it, because the speaker *is* the Savior, Immanuel, "God-with-us" (how close and personal can a God get?).

The Sermon opens with the Beatitudes, and the first is not simply one of the eight but probably is to be understood as a theme statement of which the subsequent seven are elaboration and from which the remainder of the Sermon is derived. "Blessed are the poor in spirit, for theirs is the kingdom of heaven [=kingdom of God]." Consider that a presentation of *prescriptive* law would *have* to open: "Blessed are the rich in moral ability, for they shall be able to attain (if not *create*) the kingdom of God." Yet this is precisely what Jesus does *not* say! His purpose is quite the contrary: The kingdom is God's *gift* to those who in their poverty know that they have not the wherewithal (including the ability to love) for bringing in or even meriting entrance into God's kingdom. The commandments that follow, then, which mark out a life-style of unprecedented moral heroism, represent a description of what God offers to make possible to the poor who will accept and step out upon the promise of that even now available kingdom.

Now who among us would presume (or even desire) to bypass that Beatitude and approach the Sermon as a prescription to be undertaken in his own strength? Or who, once he has heard the promise involved, even would desire that the commandments be scaled down, made more "realistic," adjusted toward the level of actual human performance? Of course, when the matter is put this way, no Christian would raise his hand. And yet the new morality is in rebellion against "law" (including Sermon on the Mount law), and its tendency is to adjust moral teachings to the level of actual human performance. But the explanation is not that the new moralists are anti-Christian or men of evil intent; it is simply that they have not heard (or heard sufficiently) the promise of the kingdom.

The rebellion, though justified, is misdirected (as rebellions tend to get). "Law" is not the villain; "prescription," the perverted understanding of it, is. Let us in all fervor join the new morality in throwing out this evil spirit; but if we do not put the good spirit of *descriptive* law in its place, it is sure to come back on us with seven other spirits more evil than itself. (I know that the new moralists deny that their desire is to eliminate all law, and we will speak to that point in a moment; but I still maintain that the *effect* of the new morality is to undercut the role of law.)

But the proper sort of law properly understood and administered is no threat to freedom any more than true authority, as opposed to Grand Inquisitor-type authoritarianism, is. In fact, proper law—and particularly God's law—can be a very real guarantee and source of freedom. The law that commands all the cars on one side of the freeway to go in the same direction is precisely what creates our freedom to drive on freeways—and I, for one, would not want to trust simply upon the loving impulses of my fellow drivers in this case. And if I might jump to a topic which is still several chapters ahead of us, my conviction is that the presence of a moral law which confines sex to the marriage bed in the long run will create a people who are really and truly more personally and sexually free than where there is no such law.

"But there are EXCEPTIONS!"

I know! I know! I've been around the new morality enough to have heard the line before. Publicly, the new morality claims to recognize only the one great law of love. Actually, there is one other great law that is just as crucial, namely, "To every rule there are EXCEPTIONS." The problem, however, is whether it is the case that the exception *proves* the rule or *destroys* it. So we had better talk about "exceptions."

Now contrary to the general impression, the new morality did neither invent nor discover the principle of "exceptions." I would guess that there never has been a moral or civil or ritual code—no matter how rigid, legalistic, or prescriptive—that has not allowed for the possibility of special circumstances that justify exceptions. For instance, Roman Catholic law forbids divorce; the decree is absolute, but there are ways . . . There are ways of legally dissolving marriages without calling it divorce. Again, I do not know how the law reads or whether it even covers such eventualities, but everyone knows that there are circumstances under which speed limits fairly may be ignored and under which the police actually will help you break them.

New moralists in general protest their high regard for our inherited moral standards and traditions as representing counsel and guidance that incorporate true wisdom for the moral life. However, they are quick to proceed, there are EXCEPTIONS. Obviously; the proposition is unarguable; every Christian morality ever devised has recognized their presence. The question, then, does not concern the theory but the practical matter of how exceptions are to be handled. Are they, as has been the case with all the old moralities, to be mentioned in the last chapter, printed in lower case—if not as an appendix, in minuscule? Or are they, as with the new morality, to be introduced in the first chapter, in capital letters, and made the theme of every chapter thereafter?

New-morality books tend to become collections of stories in which the author exercises his talent for gathering or dreaming up exceptional situations to which the normal rules do not apply. In so doing it would seem that these writers inadvertently are betraying certainly their protestations of respect for moral law and probably their own good intentions as well, because such an array of stories inevitably suggests that exceptional circumstances requiring the suspension of normal morality are as common as old shoes (to put an old metaphor to new use). Certainly it is an accurate adage that "the exception proves the rule," but there is a limit; once exceptions become the order of the day, then there is no more rule, and the situations in which it *does* apply become the exceptions. How many exceptions can a poor rule (or even a good rule) take?

Also, this penchant for recounting exception stories becomes an invitation. If the reader goes to work and exercises his talent, he probably can find exceptional circumstances surrounding any moral decision he faces; all it takes is a little imagination. It may be nothing more than that he is *exceptionally* bored on the one hand and feels an *exceptional* lust for a certain girl on the other, but particularly if the word "lust" can be enunciated "love" (and it doesn't take much of a slur to do it), then feel free! Although I am aware that such is not the conscious intent of most new moralists, this is where things tend to come out: "how to *feel* free while *making* free"—with the help of *the exception.*

My understanding of "the exception" I derived (along with all the rest of my understandings) from Søren Kierkegaard, he being one of the few thinkers who has given careful and deliberate attention to this concept. In his book entitled *Fear and Trembling* (which title is itself of utmost significance as regards the point to which we would speak) he broaches the problem "Is there such a thing as a teleological suspension of the ethical?"—which is simply a fancied-up way of asking, "Could there be situations in which God calls a man to do something which under normal circumstances would be considered immoral?" The situation that was bothering Kierkegaard at the time was this: (By the way, here appears the first distinction between Kierkegaard and the new morality; he was "bothered" by the idea of exceptions; the new morality takes it in stride if not actually hunting it out.) He was convinced that the Christian has a moral obligation to marry when the proper opportunity presents itself. He had met the girl whom he very much wanted as a wife; she wanted him; and they were engaged. Then Kierkegaard became possessed by the idea that God was calling him to break off the engagement and remain unmarried. That would be unethical, and yet God required it. What to do?

Although this was the exceptional case that actually was bugging Kierkegaard, the one he discussed was God's command that Abraham sacrifice (murder) his son Isaac. Here, in even more impressive fashion, morality says one thing and God says another. What to do?

It is perhaps instructive that the new morality has never shown any interest in this sort of exception in which the situation directs one to act completely contrary to his natural impulses and desires; it prefers stories in which the exceptional circumstances invite one to be free. But Kierkegaard makes it clear that to become "an exception" is about the scariest thing that can happen to a person. It places upon him an almost impossible weight of responsibility. Who am I to take responsibility for waiving the moral wisdom of the ages? Can I be sure that the situation is all that exceptional? If I am wrong, what damage have I done to myself, to the other person, to the moral structure of society? The chances are (by the simple logic of the fact that the moral law is a law) that it *does* apply in this instance; what gives me the right to say that my situation is all that much different?

Kierkegaard also points out that to claim the role of the

exception is to lose all moral security. As long as I play it by the rather clear guidance of Christian moral law as found in the New Testament and taught by the church I can be confident that I am not too far wrong; I have the backing of the experience and wisdom of some of the best people of history, of the saints and apostles, of the created order, of God himself. But if I decide that I am an exception to whom the rules do not apply, then I have none of that support; I am on my own. Perhaps I *have* received a command from God that goes contrary to what he has willed for man in general, but that "perhaps" is a very risky thing upon which to stake one's existence. Perhaps the circumstances in which I find myself are so exceptional that the command to love is the only thing that offers any guidance, but this again leaves me alone in a trackless waste at midnight carrying only this little light of mine— let it shine, let it shine, let it shine! To become "the exception" is about the scariest thing that possibly could happen to a person.

One time I was participating in a symposium on the new morality and attempted to inject something of Kierkegaard's concept of "the exception." But before I could get it well explained, a college boy who apparently had never experienced fear and trembling broke in to exclaim that he rather liked to think that he *is* an exception. I didn't know whether to laugh or to bawl.

But when you come right down to it, I am with him. I would *like* to think that this college kid—and all his kindred—were exceptional enough that they could make it simply on moral instinct rather than moral law. I would *like* to think that *I* was that exceptional. I would *like* to think that being an exception always entailed exceptional privileges and never exceptional responsibilities. I would *like* to think that I could take the exceptions and let someone else cover the risks. I would *like* to think that I could claim the independence of the exception when it suited my fancy and still claim the security of society when I wanted it. I would *like* to think . . . man, I would *like* to think no end of things. The trouble is that what the truth *forces* me to think bears absolutely no relationship to what I would *like* to think. Far be it from me to contradict old songs, but the truth is that wishing—even if done upon a star—will *not* make it so.

And this brings us right to the heart of my quarrel with the new morality; it is *unrealistic*. That maneuver is what is called "hoisting someone with his own petard"—because the new moralists like to call other people's moralities unrealistic for not recognizing how exceptional how many situations are how much of the time. There is nothing—nothing at all—wrong with the *theory* of the new morality; it is simply that it overlooks the practical truth of how people operate. Kierkegaard again (it is not that I do not believe that there have been other worthwhile thinkers in history; it is just that he and I have a sort of agreement by which he gets the credit due him and I am saved the work of reading a bunch of other authors) is the one who goes to the pith of the thing. He was discussing, not the new morality, but the way in which Lutheranism handles the balance between faith and works so that works tend continually to get dropped out. He says: "Lutheranism is excellent; it is truth. In regard to this excellent Lutheranism I have only one misgiving. My misgiving does not concern Lutheranism—no, it concerns myself. I am convinced that I am not an honest soul but a cunning fellow."[2]

I suppose that honest souls such as my college friend of the symposium are exceptional enough that they can navigate life on love alone; the rest of us cunning fellows such as Kierkegaard and I need the help and discipline that only law can give. Elsewhere Kierkegaard said (I can't for the life of me locate the passage, so if it should turn out that *he* didn't say it, *I* will) that our natural inclination is to be strict with others and lenient with our-

[2] *For Self-Examination*, trans. Howard and Edna Hong (Minneapolis: Augsburg Publishing House, 1940), p. 22.

selves, whereas Christianity asks us to be lenient with others and strict with ourselves. The new morality prefers the
first option. New moralists do not find the possibility of
many of these famed "exceptions" when it comes to administrations running colleges, governments running the
draft, communities running race relations. They see the
moral law as being rather clear and fixed in these areas;
it is only when one gets into matters of personal comport-
ment (and personal desire) that every second situation
turns out to be an exception.

In refusing to allow the entirely valid recognition of exceptions to be used in such a way as to undercut the necessary role of law, we are pointing toward a third concept,
"discipline." It is the case here as with "authority" and
"law" earlier in our discussion. The fact is that these concepts often have been perverted in practice. Revolt against
the perversions is proper and in order, but it is tragic that
it should seem necessary for the revolt to carry away the
true and valuable understandings as well.

There is no denying that discipline is a concept central
to the New Testament understanding of the Christian life.
Hebrews 12:5–11 is the golden passage—in which the
matter is put as clearly and unequivocally as possible: "God
is treating you as sons; for what son is there whom his
father does not discipline? If you are left without discipline, in which all have participated, then you are illegitimate children and not sons." Here is a text to which followers of the new morality and all modern Christians
might well give a little attention.

It can't be any other way. When the command of love
and the promise of the kingdom are spelled out in the
moral teachings of Scripture, one is challenged to a way of
life so highly demanding and so precision-honed that only
a rather strict discipline will afford hope of accomplishing
it.

"As a father disciplines his children, so does the

Lord . . .": Here is the key. There is one who has the right to discipline the Christian—and only one. This is the Lord, who has the right by virtue of the fact that he also is *the* authority regarding the Christian life. Indeed, "authority" and "discipline" are very much correlative terms, if not almost synonymous.

God, ultimately, is the only one qualified to administer the discipline of Christian morality. But when one man (or group of men) takes it upon himself to set up and enforce a discipline for other men, this is when trouble arises and the stage is set for the sort of revolt that is represented by the new morality. (Nonetheless, by this statement we do not intend to prohibit men a role in the discipline of their fellows.) But there is no true discipline unless it is backed by true authority; and no man has the requisites for being moral authority for another.

Christian discipline is God's discipline; it also is intended to be self-discipline. This is not a contradiction in terms, because "self-discipline" is itself both an impossible concept and yet a necessary one. Consider that "self-discipline" cannot mean what it says, the discipline of doing what the self directs at the moment. To act simply upon the directives of the self in its immediacy is precisely the contrary of what we mean by "discipline." Discipline must represent that which comes from other than self or is more than self (even if it be a decision that past self has made in order to control present self). Kierkegaard made this point very persuasively, but we will not be so tiresome as to mention the fact here.

What we really mean by self-discipline, then, is *voluntary* as against *imposed* discipline. A voluntary discipline is one I willingly have accepted for myself and which, in the long run, I truly *want* to obey even if, in the moment, my wants run quite contrary.

And the Christian discipline is nothing if not a voluntary discipline. God, being who he is, just does not force people to be Christian; and men *can't* force other men to be Christian (not that they don't work at it; they may force them to join churches, to endure rituals, to recite creeds, but they can't force them to be Christians). It should be obvious that Christianity's descriptive law is a direct corollary of the voluntariness of its discipline and that, conversely, prescriptive law and imposed discipline fit together as hand and glove. Indeed, a Christian almost could be defined as one who voluntarily has put himself under God's discipline in Christ, for in effect this is the significance of the earliest Christian confession, "Jesus is Lord."

In the Christian discipline, the "disciple" (we tend to forget the derivation of that word, don't we?) is answerable directly to God and only to him; but this does not mean that he can't use the help of other men in the process. In fact, if he takes the teachings of Jesus as a primary locus of God's moral discipline and goes to the Scriptures to find those teachings, he already has used the help of other men, namely the biblical authors and, for that matter, the entire community of faith that preserved and interpreted the tradition.

This brings us to a point of marked contrast between the new morality and the ethic of promise. If the new morality holds any concept of discipline at all (which certainly in the final analysis it must) it would by the nature of the case be a very highly individualized discipline—in order to cover the multitude of exceptions, if for no other reason. The ethic of promise, however, does its teaching within the context of the community of faith which is the church. After all, "the kingdom of God" is itself a communal concept, applying in the present to a somewhat circumscribed community (those who have accepted the kingly rule of God) but moving toward the future community of man (when God and his kingly rule shall be all in all). Ours is a community discipline—a church discipline, if you will.

We must be very careful at this point. "Church discipline" has become a naughty word—and with no little justification. However, in our terms church discipline cannot intend a discipline set up by the institution and imposed on its constituency; we already have outlawed any such. But the church is a community of those who have become a community precisely on the basis of their common recognition of Jesus as Lord and thus their common acceptance of his discipline. Church discipline, then, is not a case of the church disciplining one of its members but of a person's brethren helping him remain true to the discipline he voluntarily accepted and still professes. The church has no right to take over God's disciplining function; it can perform an invaluable function in reminding, counseling, warning, and even reprimanding the Christian in a way that will help to keep him under the firm but loving hand of the one whom he voluntarily confesses as Father.

To comment upon the mechanics of how the Christian community should be structured and what procedures it should use in this function of church discipline would take us beyond the scope of this book. But although it is a topic virtually unmentioned in contemporary treatments of morality, there is no more vital issue nor one more relevant to the moral crisis we confront.

What we here have discussed as "discipline"—God's discipline, whether mediated through the Scriptures, the church community, and/or the direct action of the Holy Spirit—necessarily will be what, in our opening chapter, we specified under the early Christian nomenclature as an "arcane (hidden) discipline." This discipline, oriented as it is toward the demand of love perfectionism, is simply too rigorous and high-reaching to be either possible or desirable in the eyes of natural man. The Christian is willing to put himself under it only because it is *God's* discipline and because, being his, it can be accepted as including also his promise of the gift that makes the demand possible, the promise of the kingdom to which God irrev-

ocably is committed and at which even now he is hard
at work.

But this promise is just what the world has not heard,
has chosen not to hear. It cannot be expected, therefore,
that this discipline will appeal to the world; it must be
followed by the Christian as a hidden discipline, one that
makes sense only within his own context. Those, then,
who share with the Apostle Paul the conviction that "the
foolishness of God is wiser than men, and the weakness of
God stronger than men" will not be too discomfited to
find their moral idealism being mocked as unrealistic, pi-
etistic, irrelevant to men in a world come of age, for they
know "in whom they have believed and are persuaded that
he is able."

But with this emphasis on "authority," "law," and "discipline," what has happened to the *desideratum* of "freedom"? Let us speak to the topic just once more.

It may well be that the ethic of promise is more truly
deserving of the characterization "freedom" than the new
morality is. There is an ambiguity in the term which must
be exposed. Karl Barth once said, "Man does the good
when he acts according to the imperative inherent in the
gift of freedom. He does evil when he obeys a law that is
contrary to his freedom."[3] The good action is one which
manifests and promotes freedom; the evil action one which
denies and hampers it. Barth would seem to be siding with
the farthest-out of the new moralists, making company
with the likes of Hugh Hefner and Timothy Leary. Yet in
reality Barth stands a pole away; the difference comes in
what is meant by "freedom."

An illustration may help get us to the crux of the matter.
Put a subject in front of a table upon which are an assort-
ment of pills—all sorts, shapes, sizes, and colors—and tell
him to be free. Put a second subject at the table; but tell

[3] "The Gift of Freedom," in *The Humanity of God* (Richmond, Va.:
John Knox Press, 1960), p. 84.

him not to eat the red ones, they are poison and could kill him. Which of the two men is the freer?

Of course, it all depends upon what you mean by "freedom." The first subject can make his choices without any sort of restraint, without there being any bias in the situation; what he does is entirely up to him, he is free to act simply on the basis of his own wisdom and determination. In the second situation there has been introduced law ("Don't eat the red pills"), authority (the word of the man who has reason to know what red pills will do), and discipline (the subject must restrain himself from eating some attractive-looking pills).

What the first subject has, obviously, is freedom *from;* he truly is under fewer restraints than the second man. However, equally obviously, his freedom is precarious and perilous; one mistake and all his freedom is forever forfeited. What the second subject has is freedom *to* and freedom *for.* Precisely because of the help he receives from authority, law, and discipline, he is free *to* live and develop as a person; he is free *for* productive labor and service to his fellow men.

And so Barth's statement—although intending something quite contrary to what the new morality teaches—is an accurate reflection of the role freedom plays in the ethic of promise, for Barth makes it abundantly clear that for him "it is God who determines how human freedom becomes directive and criterion for human action."

We have talked now of authority, of law, of discipline. Our hope is that these have been discovered to be not in conflict with love, not even in tension with love, but as the very channels through which God's love accomplishes its work in the world. Indeed, our hope is that love can be seen as more loving when it stands in company with these more rigorous elements than when it stands alone. It may be that nothing we have said in this chapter stands in outright contradiction to the new morality. There may be new moralists who would claim that their understand-

ing of love has assumed these accompaniments of authority, law and discipline. But if so, it will have done no harm
to bring to inspection these assumptions which the new
morality has glossed over if not omitted.

8

In Defense of Liberty

To this point we have been developing the general theory of the ethic of promise and have not done much by way of giving it specific application. The remainder of the book will be devoted to overcoming that lack—although it must be said that even here we are not attempting anything like blanket coverage. There are many important ethical and moral issues to which we will not so much as speak. The ones we choose are those to which the eschatological perspective seems particularly relevant, those perhaps which tend to get slighted in many discussions, and above all, those about which I can think of something to say.

Undoubtedly the greatest moral problem of our time— and probably all times—is violence. "Violence" may not be a big enough word to take in all we have in mind; our concern has to do with any and all ways in which some people forcibly restrain other people from exercising their full liberty as persons. Such restraint, of course, can be applied economically, psychologically, in any number of ways other than just physical brutality. If the term "violence" can include these, well and good. In any case, under this larger heading physical brutality forms a sizable section, and under the heading of physical brutality the major issue is that of war. Because this is the way the problem is built, our discussion on the pages to follow will tend to focus on the specific of war—but only as a critical test case regarding violence per se. Most of what we say will have relevance to the broader issue, and our desire is that the total problem constantly be borne in mind.

Our first essay at the matter—constituting the remainder of this chapter—appeared a few years ago as a *Christian Century* article; it had been written some time before that. Thereby hangs a tale—a tale which really ought not be told, although my obsession about honesty leaves me no recourse. Once upon a time I wrote the article and submitted it to the *Century*. Once upon another time shortly thereafter it came back to me with a printed rejection slip. I put the manuscript in my file to mellow, hoping that the *Century* would do the same. I waited a few years, sent in the manuscript again, and had it accepted. Thus this, my first contribution to the *Century*, was the sixth to appear. I have great faith in *The Christian Century*, and sometimes it has paid off (that is, my faith has, not the *Century*).

Here proposed is a theology of non-resistance. Let it be said at the outset that *a theology of* non-resistance is not the same thing as *the case for* non-resistance. Rather, the following proceeds from the profound conviction that the only adequate basis for a truly Christian pacifism must come from a committed reading of the New Testament, must signify obedience to Christ's teaching and counsel. Theological explanations come later. But since the human mind seeks to understand that which it is called upon to obey, it is proper to set forth a theology of non-resistance and use rational constructs to fill in behind first-order convictions of faith.

Having relegated theological arguments to a second place, arguments of prudence now are to be relegated to no place at all. More often than not, pacifism is sold as a social and political technique. It is asserted that ways of peace would be more effective in attaining our national goals than ways of war ever could be, that love can do everything war can do and do it better. This may well be true in most if not all situations. But for a Christian to propose this as the ground of his position is to betray his own intention. For he thus has moved the question into the realm of casuistry, has sacrificed any ultimate appeal to religious *principle* in the interest of arguing *cases*. He has, in effect, deserted his religious authority and given the matter over to the political scientists and statesmen. And although these gentlemen's findings today should support the view that non-resistance is the more effective technique, there always remains the live possibility that under the altered circumstances of tomorrow the findings might honestly point to a different conclusion. Considerations of expediency well may recommend a policy of peace, and Christian pacifists of course are happy when competent social scientists come to this view. But such a finding is in no sense the basis for a specifically religious, or Christian, position.

In this connection, the term "non-resistance" seems preferable to "pacifism." "Non-resistance" has biblical rootage in Jesus' "Do not resist one who is evil" (Matthew 5:39); and the very word "pacifism" has come to suggest the argument of expediency, the use of love as a calculated technique for achieving social and political goals.

Having then, for present purposes, disavowed all prudential arguments, let us proceed to a theology proper. Actually, the distance between a Christian pacifist and a Christian non-pacifist is not so great as might appear. ("Non-pacifist" is an awkward enough term, to be sure; but on the other hand, it is manifestly unjust to refer to all who are not pacifists as "militarists.") No Christian takes joy in war; the non-pacifist is as much "against" war as is the pacifist. In extreme cases, however, the non-pacifist feels bound to affirm that liberty—which itself is just as much one of God's good gifts as is peace—is of such value that it must be preserved even at the cost of war. And the Christian certainly will figure the "cost of war" as much in terms of the damage he will be forced to inflict as in terms of that he will have to suffer.

The theology here proposed steals a march on the non-pacifist (to use a military metaphor) by building upon the very same principle; namely, that liberty is of such value that it must be preserved whatever the cost. This statement only can mean that there are *certain liberties* which must be preserved; for it is obvious that liberty in the abstract is so vague as hardly to be defendable and equally obvious that men are quite willing to sacrifice certain liberties precisely that they may defend certain others. In reality, then, each man holds a scale of liberties (perhaps, or probably, without being aware of it) and is willing to sacrifice any and all the liberties below a given point in order to preserve those that lie above. Thus—to use an illustration that contrasts a very low liberty with a very high one and so makes the distinction easy—during World War II we were willing to forego the liberty of indulging our taste for sugar in the interests of preserving the higher liberty of national existence. Toward the top of any person's scale surely would lie the liberties guaranteed in the Bill of Rights. Probably most Christians would be willing to sacrifice their liberty to vote if this were the only way they could preserve freedom of worship; and so on.

In most cases the liberty that stands at the top of the scale, the freedom for which one would be willing to sacrifice every other, is the fundamental freedom of living, simply of staying alive. For many men, however, and particularly for Christians, this top-ranked freedom must be further defined; these people are willing to sacrifice their own lives in order to preserve the freedom of living for others, whether those "others" be thought of as humanity, the nation, the family back home, or the buddies in the foxhole.

Clearly too, on this scale of liberties each non-pacifist —and, theoretically, each "prudential pacifist" as well— has a point at which he would be willing even to go to war in order to preserve the liberties above that point. Of course, in view of the Christian assessment of the cost of war, that point will be high up indeed.

Positively the only thing wrong with this scale-of-liberties thinking as used by the non-pacifist is that it overlooks a liberty which the Christian must put at the very top; namely, man's ultimate liberty, for which he should be willing to sacrifice all others. But strangely enough, this is a liberty which need not and indeed cannot be defended by war; and what is even more strange, the very act of going to war marks its loss.

The argument here builds upon a conception of the nature of man (and of God) that is not uncommon in modern theology, but which I have derived most directly from such men as Søren Kierkegaard, Martin Buber, Emil Brunner, and Hugh Vernon White. Man fundamentally is to be understood as a spiritual person (or a personal spirit), whereas God is understood as *the* spiritual Person. "Personhood" (a more awkward but much more accurate term than "personality") is constituted in one's *actions* as a free moral agent. A person acts within a real, concrete, living milieu, and in his acting he makes choices—not only in the simple sense of deciding between two offered alternatives but in the more complex sense of creating and molding new alternatives and higher syntheses. Therefore the "person" in his actions is, above all, free; he is responsible and answerable. The integrity of his action is such that he must be considered as an entity complete and whole in himself, never as a part or particular within a larger system.

This is not to overlook or deny that man is dependent upon God, that he becomes a true person only as he recognizes and lives within this dependency—even though the acceptance of the relationship is a free act on his part. Just as the baby becomes a human being in response to and imitation of the human beings who confront him, so men become true persons only as they respond positively to the confrontation of the spiritual Person, God. This positive response we call "faith," and in the faith relationship is found a person-to-Person communion, an I-Thou fellowship, in which the two spirits coinhere without loss of personal identity. They remain distinct but not separate.

On the other hand, a negative response to God's confrontation, in which the human person asserts his freedom in the face of God, in defiance, disobedience, and disdain —this response we call "sin." And it results in alienation and disharmony, in "distance" between God and man.

From the foregoing it follows that man's ultimate liberty is precisely this freedom to become a true person—to respond to God in faith, to know even as one is known. If need be, the Christian will relinquish every other liberty in the interests of preserving this one, for "if the Son [i.e., the One in whom the Christian confronts God] makes you free, you will be free indeed" (John 8:36).

Observe, in the first place, that this freedom cannot be threatened by evil men and therefore need not and cannot be defended through war. Though a man be imprisoned, tortured, deprived of all his customary liberties, his freedom of access to God is not touched. If he be killed— Paul says that it actually is better to depart and be with Christ, and Jesus assures us that we need not fear those who kill the body but cannot kill the soul.

In theory at least, there is one way in which a human oppressor could threaten this ultimate liberty. If he suppressed religion so successfully that children grew up without knowledge of the gospel, then their freedom of access to God would seem to be abrogated. Historically, however, things have not worked in this fashion. "The blood of the martyrs is the seed of the church." Godless regimes never have proved an insurmountable obstacle to the spread of the gospel. Warfare may be effective in preserving other liberties, but it is neither necessary nor useful in preserving man's ultimate liberty.

Is there, then, any quarter from which this liberty can be threatened? Is it possible for this liberty to be lost? Yes; a man himself, through his own sin, can and does destroy his freedom of personal access to God. And there is one manner of sinning through which this loss of freedom becomes acute. Whenever I deny or fail to respect the personhood of another man, I effectually deny my own personhood. I cannot be in a positive relationship to God while refusing another the possibility of that same relationship. "If anyone says, 'I love God,' and hates his brother, he is a liar; for he who does not love his brother whom he has seen, cannot love God whom he has not seen" (1 John 4:20).

To treat another as though he were anything less than a person (in the fullest meaning of that term) is, of course, a sin against that man. But even more it is (like all sin) a sin against God; for consider the lengths to which God has gone, the price he has paid in enabling that man to become a person. Through creation, God endowed that man (as he did me) with the freedom, the positive capabilities, and all the gifts that make personhood possible. And God gave his only Son for that man (as he gave him for me) in order that that man might become a true person. To recognize a man's personhood, then, actually means to recognize him as "a brother for whom Christ died." To fail to respect this identification is to fail to respect God in his greatest act; it is, in effect, to deny the efficacy of Christ in one's own case and thus one's own relationship to God.

So I impair the ultimate freedom of mankind every time I fail to respect the other man as a person, every time I fail to honor him as a brother for whom Christ died. And since military warfare is the human institution in which men are treated least like persons, it follows that war—no

matter how effective it may be in preserving lesser liberties
—inevitably destroys our ultimate liberty.

In this view, the final evil of war does not lie specifically
in what is done to the enemy. It is quite conceivable that one
man could take another's life while still respecting him as
a person. Such certainly would be the case in so-called
"mercy killings," and it might be argued that gunning down
a homicidal maniac ultimately works for his own good as
well as the good of society. No, the basic evil of war lies
in the estimate of other persons which it demands from and
engenders in us.

"But," the non-pacifist may object, "this is a misunderstanding of war. Hate is not a necessary nor even desirable
concomitant. The soldier who fights coolly, objectively, doing it as a job that has to be done, is a much better soldier
than the recruit who becomes emotionally involved, who
sees red and feels hot hatred toward the enemy."

If "hate" is thus narrowly defined, the ultimate evil of
war is not even in the hatred it arouses. In fact, from the
viewpoint we are developing, hate is less insidious than
this "cold objectivity"; hate is at least a "personal" relationship (although inverted), whereas cold objectivity means
precisely to treat the other man as though he were a thing
rather than a person.

A concrete example will make graphic this impersonalization that lies at the heart of war. In Ernest Hemingway's
For Whom the Bell Tolls, Robert Jordan, the American
volunteer who is directing the dynamiting of a strategic
bridge, discusses the operation with old Anselmo, one of
the Spanish republican guerrillas.

> "You have killed?" Robert Jordan asked in the inti-
> macy of the dark and of their day together.
> "Yes. Several times. But not with pleasure. To me it is
> a sin to kill a man. Even Fascists whom we must kill.
> . . . I am against all killing of men."

"Yet you have killed."

"Yes. And will again. But if I live later, I will try to live in such a way, doing no harm to anyone, that it will be forgiven."

"By whom?"

"Who knows? Since we do not have God here any more, neither His Son nor the Holy Ghost, who forgives? I do not know."

"You have not God any more?"

"No. Man. Certainly not. If there were God, never would He have permitted what I have seen with my eyes. . . . But with or without God, I think it is a sin to kill. To take the life of another is to me very grave. . . ."

"To win a war we must kill our enemies. That has always been true."

"Clearly. In war we must kill. But I have rare ideas," Anselmo said. . . .

"We will be together," Robert Jordan told him. "I will tell you what there is to do at all times."

"Then there is no problem," Anselmo said. "I can do anything that I am ordered."

. . . [Robert Jordan ponders the conversation.] There is not you, and there are no people that things must not happen to. Neither you nor this old man is anything. You are instruments to do your duty. There are necessary orders that are no fault of yours and there is a bridge and that bridge can be the point on which the future of the human race can turn. As it can turn on everything that happens in this war. You have only one thing to do and you must do it. . . .

[Later, at the time of the dynamiting itself, Robert Jordan instructs Anselmo on how he is to pick off the bridge sentry.] "When thou firest," Robert Jordan said, "take a rest and make very sure. Do not think of it as a man but as a target, *de acuerdo?* Do not shoot at the whole man but at a point. Shoot for the exact center of

the belly—if he faces thee. At the middle of his back if
he is looking away. . . ."

"I will do as thou orderest," Anselmo said.

"Yes. I order it thus," Robert Jordan said.

I'm glad I remembered to make it an order, he thought.
That helps him out. That takes some of the curse off. I
hope it does, anyway. Some of it. . . .[1]

Anselmo here gives expression to a revulsion toward war
that must be natural to every Christian; and though the
conclusion regarding God's absence is wrong, his is a true
instinct: The atrocities of war hardly can represent God's
will. Robert Jordan, on the other hand, gives voice to the
logic, the psychology, by which Christians overcome their
revulsion to the point that they conscientiously can participate in war.

War becomes possible to a Christian only as he considers himself an "instrument to do his duty" and considers
the enemy a "target," not a whole man but a point to be
shot at. How subtly and yet how inevitably these impersonal
thought forms take over is well illustrated by Paul Ramsey's
Century article in defense of U.S. policy in Vietnam.
Whether consciously or subconsciously, I submit that, as a
Christian ethicist, Ramsey felt uncomfortable in defending
"war" and so shifted his terminology to talk about "arbi-
tration [or even *arbitrament*] of arms." And what is an
arbitrament of arms, for goodness' sake? It is a couple of
old-fashioned gallants covered all over from head to toe,
covered all over with steel ring-o-lets, riding at each other
with staves until one falls off his horse; whereupon the victor
alights to help the vanquished to his feet and leads him to
the castle where they can continue their arbitrament over a
bowl of mead. "War," everybody knows, is hell; but an
"arbitrament of arms"—now there is a concept at which
even the nicest Christian need not blanch!

[1] The passage from *For Whom the Bell Tolls,* by Ernest Hemingway,
is reprinted by special permission of Charles Scribner's Sons.

But this way of thinking is a denial of that freedom which is worth much more than all the freedoms that may be preserved in consequence. In the first place, men are persons and will remain so regardless of how we choose to view them. Thinking of them as instruments and targets does not make them so. And war is war—nothing else—and getting more that way all the time. But to even greater point: What insult is it to the other man, what damage to my personal relationship to him and to God, what affront to that God who has given his only Son that both I and my enemy might become true persons, when I deliberately suspend my Christian understanding in order to consider men as mere things.

Yet this is what war does and must do. In what conflict may come, the only expediency that will enable an American Christian to launch a missile wiping out hundreds of thousands of men, women, and children is that he will not have to aim the missile at *persons*—not even a city. His aim will be simply to hit a *target,* only to direct a radar blip to a given set of co-ordinates. So far can persons be impersonalized.

Hemingway's Robert Jordan also presents the reasoning that makes Christians willing to accept these exigencies of war: "There is a bridge and that bridge can be the point on which the future of the human race can turn." But if our faith is right that God and God alone is the lord of history, then is it not somewhat presumptuous for man to claim the prescience to recognize the turning points of history, the wisdom to see what must be done at that point, and the authority to take the matter into his own hands? Can it conceivably be the will of God that his holy intentions for man and history be accomplished by man's renouncing the Christian estimate of persons?

Of course one dare not base an argument on what might have happened if what did happen hadn't; yet it is plain that numerous battles and wars in which participating Christians considered victory crucial for the future of the race were in fact *lost*—and lost without jeopardizing the race or frustrating God's purposes for it. The Christian's responsibility is to act in obedience and faith; it is God's responsibility to oversee history and its turning points.

"All of this is well and good," the non-pacifist may reply, "but it overlooks one very painful dilemma. If when one nation overruns another I stand by and do nothing, I actually am treating the victims as less than persons in the interests of treating the oppressors as persons. If, for instance, because of non-resistant principles I allow the Vietcong to take over, I am in effect impersonalizing the South Vietnamese."

This argument at best is only half true. To refuse to come to the military defense of the victim *could* be a sign of unconcern, but it is not inevitably so. The Christian pacifist is obliged to do everything possible in behalf of the victim—short of treating the oppressors as less than persons. He will bring to bear all appropriate political and moral suasions in the effort to prevent the oppression; he will use every opportunity to minister to the victim in the way of sympathetic concern, moral support, relief, and rehabilitation; he will pray unceasingly in behalf of both victim and oppressor. Surely such an attitude and such activity cannot be classified as personal unconcern and irresponsibility. Indeed, the Christian pacifist and non-pacifist part ways only at the point of war and preparation for war; their political and social activity can be in concert up to that point.

War is out of order because of the impersonalization it fosters. But, it might be objected, this impersonalization is the mark of many other institutions as well—business, labor, public education, mass communications, government, etc. True; and the Christian must be alert to the threat wherever it appears in our social life. But the difference is this: These other institutions need not be impersonalizing; the Christian can and will work at *reforming* them. War, however, is an institution whose very existence depends on man's ability to impersonalize. *Reform* is out of the question. Thus the Christian is obliged to work for war's *abolishment*. And until war is abolished the Christian must refuse to participate in it lest he abet the jeopardy of the one freedom that is infinitely more precious than any and all other freedoms he might defend.

9

The Blood-Drenched Robe of the Conqueror

————◆————

The only thing wrong with that article (in *my* opinion, it goes without saying) is that it was not as eschatologically oriented as the ethic of promise should be and that it could leave the impression that to refrain from violence is in effect to give up and do nothing.

This last is a misunderstanding that is endemical to our activist age: Unless a person is pushing the furniture around with considerable show and noise, he isn't *doing* anything. "Get busy, fellow, busy, busy, busy. God has no hands but our hands (as the Scripture does not say), so for God's sake do *something!"*

The lie was given to this frantic fallacy as long ago as the prophet Isaiah: "In returning and rest you shall be saved; in quietness and in trust shall be your strength" (Isaiah 30:15). There are situations in which the most helpful thing man can do is to hold still, quiet down, stay calm, and sit tight so that God can do the doing *he* has in mind. The idea that man has to beat God out of bed each morning and be out there building the old kingdom is just plain heresy.

However, out of deference to the age we will attempt to show that non-resisting evil actually is a very positive form of endeavor, one indeed that amounts to nothing less than *conquest*. Also, we will get our train of thought properly eschatologized.

The truth is that there is already in that *Century* article much more of an eschatological orientation than meets the eye—although I didn't see it at the time of writing either. But the talk about the ultimate liberty of becoming a true person is very much to the point, for this liberty is found precisely in coming under the kingly rule of God (although we did not use that phraseology) and the consummated kingdom adequately could be described as humanity's finding of such liberty. Then too, the comment upon man's presumption in deciding that he must resort to violence in order to save the historical process and bring it out to God's goal is to say simply that man does not have faith in the real power of God's kingly rule, does not truly trust the promise of the kingdom.

Nevertheless, we can carry this application of the ethic of promise a step further by picking up a cue out of early Quakerism. Some of the seventeenth-century Friends promoted their non-resistant faith under a doctrine of "the Lamb's War." The Lamb who was slain, precisely by allowing himself to be slain rather than doing the slaying, has won (or is winning) a victory that shall overcome the world. Those who follow his banner, fight with him, and hope to share in his victory also will fight in the way that he fights.

I was intrigued with the idea immediately upon hearing it. Certainly it contributes the eschatological perspective which the ethic of promise wants. And it has that neat little twist about fighting in reverse, conquering by being slain, which also has the effect of making non-resistance a positive "doing something" rather than a passive "doing nothing." My only concern was that these clever old Quakers had pulled a fast march on the Revelator, for everyone knows that in the Book of Revelation the Lamb hardly wins his victory by non-resisting; a more gory and violent picture is not to be found in the Bible and scarcely in the whole of world literature. Personally, I preferred the Quaker version to the Revelator's, but there is no denying as to which of the two is scriptural.

And then, some time later, I came across the book *Time and History,* an exposition of Revelation by the contemporary Swiss scholar Matthias Rissi. Lo and behold, the antique Quakers were right all along; the battle of Armageddon turns out to be a pacifist manifesto; and the fantastic friends of Fox come off better as exegetes than we brilliant moderns do. Rissi can help us.

The Book of Revelation would seem to be adequately eschatological in its orientation, being, as it is, a poetic portrayal of the consummation, of God's final victory over evil, in which sin, death, the devil, sorrow, injustice—all that is destructive and dehumanizing—are forever done away with. Then comes the kingdom of God in its fullness, the time when all things are ordered according to his love, mercy, and holy desire.

And when, where, and how is it that the Revelator sees this tremendous victory taking place? At Armageddon, as we have supposed, where Christ appears as a Genghis Khan leading a Mongol horde of saints and angels in an orgy of slaughter, pillage, rape, and general bloodletting. No wonder peace-loving Christians (and most other sorts of Christians as well) have tended to shy away from the book.

But our first impression should be examined. The crucial victory (which, by the way, is not Armageddon) is not pictured in this way; and even the Armageddon passages are not as much this way as they usually are taken to be. The matter calls for another look.

As we shall discover on close examination, Armageddon is not depicted as a glorious, knock-down, drag-out, first-one-side-and-then-the-other fight to the finish. It is rather a picture of surrender and capitulation or, at best, mopping-up operations. Armageddon turns out to be an Appomattox Courthouse rather than a Gettysburg, the signing on the battleship USS *Missouri* rather than the dropping of the atomic bomb. Consider the text:

Then I saw heaven opened, and behold, a white horse! He who sat upon it is called Faithful and True, and in righteousness he judges and makes war. His eyes are like a flame of fire, and on his head are many diadems; and he has a name inscribed which no one knows but himself. He is clad in a robe dipped in blood, and the name by which he is called is The Word of God. And the armies of heaven, arrayed in find linen, white and pure, followed him on white horses. . . . And I saw the beast and kings of the earth with their armies gathered to make war against him who sits upon the horse and against his army. And the beast was captured, and with it the false prophet. . . .

(Revelation 19:11–14, 19–20)

Although we did skip a few verses, there is nowhere here any account of the Rider in actual combat with his enemies; this is a surrender rather than a battle scene. What we did skip, we will admit, was slighty gory—even if it was the gore of mopping up rather than of an engagement hanging in the balance. The point to which we are leading does not involve an attempt to deny that the Revelator's picture is violent. Obviously it is; yet there are some things to be said even on this score. A case can be made that all God's destructive wrath is directed against evil itself, i.e., precisely against the *enemies of mankind* rather than against mankind as such. God does not show up as one who is taking vengeance *on men*.

It is true that the Revelator shows us men being punished, but this punishment is purifying and redemptive in its effect. Indeed, Rissi amasses rather convincing evidence that the Revelator sees all men as eventually coming to Christ and into the kingdom of God. Although this is not the place to mount a detailed argument, there is reason to consider that the violence of the Revelator's picture tells us nothing at all about his understanding of the Christian love ethic and his attitude toward human violence and war.

But if Armageddon represents simply the final capitulation of evil, then when did the victory itself take place? Go back through the Book of Revelation and it becomes evident that there is nowhere recounted any sort of direct engagement between Christ the Conqueror and the forces of evil. The explanation, Rissi shows, is that the Revelator considers the victory to have been won even before his story opens; the decisive engagement had taken place at the cross of Calvary.

The key is the blood-drenched robe in which the Conqueror appears in the scene we just examined—the robe we customarily have taken as a terribly vivid symbol of bloodthirstiness. However, that robe is bloody *at the time the Conqueror appears,* before there is any possibility that the blood could have come from a battle of Armageddon (even if Armageddon had turned out to be a battle); and the Revelator knows nothing of any earlier battle in which the robe could have been bespattered with enemy blood. Yet it is the blood of victory, but also *it is the Conqueror's own.* Christ won the ultimate battle of universal history when, on the cross, he chose to be bloodied rather than to bloody his enemies. The early Quakers had it right; the outcome of history does depend upon the Lamb's War, a war in which the victory is (was) won by a being slain rather than by a slaying.

For the Revelator, Jesus' death and resurrection constitute the eschatological turning point from which will proceed and is now proceeding the kingdom of God, the final destiny of mankind and of creation itself. The crucifixion —the refusal to resist one who is evil and the willingness even to be slain out of love for the many—marks the *method* of conquest; the resurrection is the eucatastrophe marking the fact that it is *conquest,* that the Lamb who *was* slain does in fact *live* as Conqueror.

But what possible logic is there in describing the act of letting oneself be slain as "a conquest"? Perhaps this: Evil, as is the case with any invader, tries to expand its

holdings, bring more and more territory under its control.
This spread of evil takes place as one who is treated evilly
responds with some evil of his own. If my hateful act
toward you makes you hate me in return, then hatred has
conquered us both. The evil of white racism engenders the
evil of black violence, and evil has a heyday. Illustrations
could be multiplied almost as prolifically as evil multiplies
itself.

Yet Jesus—throughout his career but particularly in his
crucifixion—chose not to respond to evil by reflecting it
back into the world, thus continuing and even intensifying
its progress. No, he smothered evil by willingly interposing
himself and absorbing its trepidations into his own body.
He let evil throw its very worst against him and responded
with nothing but love. In such a situation, what could evil
do? It was like fighting fog with swords, when swords are
the only weapons evil has or knows how to use. Although
non-resistance was the very method of its accomplishment,
Jesus' was a *victory* in the truest sense of that term.

Kierkegaard has described this same economy in a very
striking metaphor.[1] He suggests that conflict and violence
are like a whirlpool, a gyration that escalates, going faster
and faster and faster until it threatens to fly apart. The
normal human response (even what passes for the Christian response) is to try to introduce into the whirl new
forces and vectors that will change the direction of spin
and bring it out to what we consider the proper conclusion,
the optimum state of affairs. However, the introduction of
new forces simply brings reaction from the forces already
present and so has the effect of kicking the swirl into even
greater turbulence.

No, the only way—the Christian way—to handle whirlpools, Kierkegaard says, is to introduce a rock, a fixed point
which has no other end in view but to stand firm and allow

[1] For an English translation of the appropriate materials and a fuller
discussion of them, see my book (why not even *buy* my book?)
Kierkegaard and Radical Discipleship (Princeton, N.J.: Princeton University Press, 1968), pp. 277–84.

the turbination to batter itself out against its own fixity. The rock, in one sense, does not resist, that is, it does not fight back; yet its willingness and ability to absorb punishment makes it something far different from what could be called "passive." It displays a courage, strength, and lasting-power which in very truth is capable of conquering the violence of whirlpools.

But coming back to the paradigm of Jesus' crucifixion, we are led to reiterate a point made in an earlier chapter: The method of non-resistance has even a ghost of a chance of working, the cross possibly can be a conquest, only because a God of resurrection capabilities stands behind the endeavor. The non-resister, obviously, runs a very high risk of getting himself wiped out; even rocks (and especially small rocks such as you and I) get rolled. But even letting oneself be wiped out can be turned to victory if the Lord of history is sponsor of the event. The way of the Lamb makes sense only on the basis of the promise of the kingdom.

According to the understanding of the Revelator, however, Jesus' death and resurrection were not an event that was over and done with in the event itself. Indeed, the entire story of the struggles and tribulations leading up to the consummated kingdom of God is presented as being the inevitable working out of that victory in which the Conqueror got his robe drenched with his own blood.

In his first appearance in the book, in the Revelator's first chapter, the heavenly Christ says: "I am the first and the last, and I am the living one; for I was dead and now I am alive for evermore, and I hold the keys of death and Hades." The implication (borne out by other passages) is very strong that the manner of his being dead and now alive is what has given him the keys. Death and Hades for the present are still running loose (which it does not take the Bible to confirm; any newspaper will do as well), but Christ already has won the keys that can and will put them behind bars.

In Chapter 5, then, the Revelator reports a vision in which a sealed scroll is presented before the heavenly throng. The scroll rather clearly represents the future, the outcome of history; and the question is posed, "Who is worthy to break the seals, to command the course of history, to bring in the kingdom as it were?" No one is found who has the authority or capability until there is introduced "the Lamb with the marks of slaughter upon him." The identification is not accidental; his volunteering for the slaughter is what has qualified him as Lord of the World and Consummator of History. And several times throughout the book appears a wording similar to the one which Handel put to such very good use: "Worthy is the Lamb that was slain . . . to receive power and riches and wisdom and strength!" The manner of his being slain is the source of his worthiness.

By speaking of "the Lamb's War," the early Quakers extended the figure to cover not only the Lamb but his followers as well. Christians take their place in the struggle and play their part in the coming of the kingdom by practicing the same means of conquest that Jesus used. The Revelator himself had not missed the implication, and the Quakers were reading their Bibles aright.

> And I heard a loud voice in heaven, saying, "Now the salvation and the power and the kingdom of our God and the authority of his Christ have come, for the accuser of our brethren has been thrown down, who accuses them day and night before our God. And they have conquered him by the blood of the Lamb and by the word of their testimony, for they loved not their lives even unto death."
>
> (Revelation 12:10–11)

Clearly, to conquer by the blood of the Lamb does not mean merely to rest secure upon what Jesus did once upon a time but to put one's own blood where he put his.

It is quite evident that the Revelator assigns a very high

value to the Christian martyrs, and our present line of thought makes it evident why. In one place he speaks of those living and yet to live, the martyrs' "brothers in Christ's service who were to be killed as they had been" (6:11 NEB). In his eleventh chapter he tells the story of the two witnesses (likely the Jewish Christian church and the Gentile Christian church) whose fate—and whose victory—is to be killed and resurrected for their testimony. And in a pivotal scene he describes the redeemed: "It is these who have not defiled themselves with women, for they are chaste; it is these who follow the Lamb wherever he goes; these have been redeemed from mankind as first fruits for God and the Lamb" (14:4). Rissi thinks the likelihood is that the author was not even considering celibacy but was drawing upon the familiar biblical analogy of unfaithfulness to God as being a whoredom. This interpretation certainly fits well with the succeeding line about following the Lamb wherever he goes; and as has been made abundantly clear, the way that the Lamb goes leads through a cross and resurrection.

Note also the most important consideration, that the significance of their redemption does not lie simply in the experience of the redeemed themselves; they are the "first fruits"—presumably of a redeemed humanity and a redeemed world. Christian morality is not just a matter of personal preference and personal consequences; it is a call to perform as first fruits for mankind at large.

If, then, Christian ethics be cast into an eschatological mode (and it is doubtful that any ethic not so cast can pass the New Testament standard of "Christian"), and if the Book of Revelation be granted its legitimate New Testament status (which it has not always enjoyed), the conclusion would seem inescapable: The victory represented in Christ's death and resurrection is a call for us to step forward and share in that victory by enlisting in the Lamb's War, following the Conqueror in the blood-drenched robe, and being willing to shed our blood in the same cause and in the same loving, sacrificial way.

There is one other point that has been made clear by the Revelator's treatment. We are dealing with much more than simply the Christian's position regarding military warfare. The Lamb's War describes a stance that applies to any and every situation in life. Precisely as far as conflict and violence have permeated human existence, just that far must the Christian follow the Lamb wherever he goes; the Lamb's victory is to be the most far-reaching conceivable.

And what goes for the Christian must go for his church as well. Indeed, unless the church as an institution demonstrates something of this same defenselessness, the willingness to risk its own martyrdom in the pursuance of its mission, there is little chance that it can raise up many individuals who will adopt the strategy for their personal lives. Where Jesus is Lord, the Lamb's War is the only one to be fought.

10
The God of the Hebrews?

━━━━━━◆◈◆━━━━━━

We have been speaking to matters of war, violence, regimentation, et al. but without speaking of politics, foreign policy, community organization, and so on. We do not deny that Christian morality (and thus the ethic of promise) will have to be involved in these areas and consequently must make hard decisions. But this is not the level on which we have chosen to speak (nor upon which, admittedly, we are qualified to speak); we have addressed ourselves to the level of the theological and religious groundings out of which these other considerations spring and by which they are guided. The one task is as valid and necessary as the other; it is simply that we have chosen the one as being ours.

As we turn now to the great moral complex that includes the problems of poverty, racism, minority rights, and so on, the same distinction obtains. In one sense this chapter will offer nothing of *practical* value, no sociopolitical analysis, no recommendations for action. Ours is simply the effort to establish *why* it is that Christians must be concerned, *what* must be the nature of their commitment. We make no claim to be handing out answers to these so very complex problems; we are striving to point to the source from which the answers are going to have to come.

In this instance the ethic of promise's source of answer, its ground of hope, can be stated very simply: The God of the kingdom is also the God of the Hebrews. That may not seem to be saying much, but we will attempt to get us a chapter in the course of doing it. Our first move is to jump backward from the Book of Revelation to the Book of Exodus.

The Hebrew word *'ibri*—which in English is transliterated as "a Hebrew"—is one of the curiosities of the Old Testament. We understand it simply as another term referring to the national-ethnic group which we also know as the children of Israel, the Israelites, and later the Jews. In time, of course, *'ibri* did come to be so used, but the evidence is that it was not originally so. A study of its appearance in the Old Testament shows it splashing backward for one occurrence in the Abraham story and splashing forward into the settlement of Canaan and even into the writings of the prophets but concentrating very definitely around Israel's stay in Egypt, i.e., in the Joseph and Moses stories.

The context in which the word is used is the first clue to its origin. Virtually without exception it comes in connection with an Israelite's relationship to the heathen. It either is a term the foreigner uses in referring to the Israelite or one the Israelite uses in referring to himself in the presence of a foreigner. It is not used within a purely Israelite situation nor within Israel's relationship to her God Yahweh. Almost certainly *'ibri* must have carried overtones of derision and/or bootlicking; it was not a term of honor, pride, or self-respect.

Not in the Bible now but in cuneiform records coming from the time of the Exodus and earlier, and gathered from scattered localities across the Fertile Crescent, there is found the word *'apiru*. It seems rather certain that the biblical word *'ibri* and the non-biblical word *'apiru* are etymologically related, although just how the derivation took place it is impossible to tell. What the wide scattering of examples does make clear is that *'apiru* does not have reference to any particular national-ethnic group; it is a non-localized word. What does appear is that the word is closely related to the legal process of selling oneself into slavery and seems to apply to one who has so sold himself or is coming to the point that he will have to.

Back to the Bible and the word *'ibri,* the suggestion correlates beautifully. In the Old Testament law, where there is reference to a man selling himself into slavery, the word *'ibri* appears; and in a couple of places, even the distinction between *'ibri* (i.e., enslaved) Israelites and non-*'ibri* Israelites becomes visible. Jeremiah 34:9 and 14 derive from the law stated in Deuteronomy 15:12 and states that "every one should set free his Hebrew slaves, male and female, so that no one should enslave a Jew, his brother." And in 1 Samuel 14, Jonathan, the son of King Saul, makes a singlehanded—and rather foolhardy—foray against a Philistine garrison. But lo and behold, a great number of people who are with the Philistines suddenly switch sides in a maneuver which verse 21 describes as follows: "Now the Hebrews who had been with the Philistines before that time and who had gone up with them into the camp, even they also turned to be with the Israelites who were with Saul and Jonathan." The story has all the indications of a slave revolt.

The evidence, then, is rather strong that in its primal setting *'ibri* was a very demeaning term applying to the very lowest strata of society—those who are so miserable and impoverished, so completely without rights or protection, that their only recourse is to sell themselves into slavery. "Scum" or "riffraff" would not be too bad a translation.[1]

Keeping in mind these overtones of the word "Hebrew," let us go back to the Exodus story to make an exciting discovery. When, at the burning bush, Yahweh commissions Moses to lead the escape from Egypt, he instructs him to "go to the king of Egypt and say to him, 'Yahweh, the God of the Hebrews, has met with us'" (Exodus 3:18). Several times thereafter, throughout the contest with Pha-

[1] For an *authoritative* discussion of the entire etymological issue, see Albrecht Alt, *Essays on Old Testament History and Religion* (Garden City, N.Y.: Doubleday Anchor Books, 1968), pp. 119–22.

raoh, Yahweh enjoins Moses and Aaron to use the phrase; it becomes a regular title. In short, *Yahweh voluntarily identifies himself with and even asks to be named as "the God of the Riffraff."* (We are not yet ready for our conclusion but can contain it no longer: Love is what God does; and what God does is identify with *Hebrews.*)

Here is *the* miracle of the Exodus—although we customarily have passed it over in favor of such comparatively empty sensations as burning bushes, staffs that go snaky (even though they are to be found in many organizations yet today), and walled water. But that the God who rightfully can claim the titles of Creator of the Universe and Lord of History should choose to be known as God of the *Hebrews*—this is simply incredible. Our upbringing has made the idea so commonplace as to rob it of its wonder; but consider that throughout human history religion always has been a luxury of the wealthy and leisured classes. It takes time and money to run a respectable religion. Temples, priests, vestments, and all the appointments don't come cheap; and if one is going to be really religious—obeying all the do's and don'ts, attending all the services, working in the ladies' aid—it soon becomes a full-time job. Hebrews need not apply.

And yet it seems obvious than any self-respecting God would be out to get the best deal he can. By rights, the God of all the earth ought to have the fanciest religion of all. "And he *asked* to be known as the God of the *Hebrews,* those miserable peons who even had to *steal* the wherewithal to build him a tent? You can't be serious!"

Ogden Nash's famous poem could do with a second verse:

> How much odder
> Of Yahwer
> To choose
> The *Hebrews!*

(OK, so it isn't such great poetry; it is beautiful theology.)

That, very clearly, *is* the God of the Exodus—and it may go a long way toward explaining some other things about him as well—maybe even how he conquers Promised Lands. The truth of the matter is that the sequence of events that begins with the escape from Egypt and concludes with the conquest of Canaan creates for Old Testament scholars a problem in historical logistics that threatens their mental equilibrium. How large a group was involved in the Exodus? If you make it big enough to pull off the conquest at the tail end of the sequence, then it is too big to be credible in the escape from Egypt and the wanderings in the wilderness. However, if you make it small enough to make the escape end of the sequence credible, you have nothing but problems with the conquest.

But the fact that Yahweh is God *of the Hebrews* may suggest an answer—and as a fringe benefit scale down the scope of his violence to make him a little more compatible with the Father of Revelation's Lamb. George Mendenhall is responsible for the suggestion.[2]

One problem with the conquest as presented in the Book of Joshua is that, although a number of pitched battles are described, there are great areas of the country which clearly wind up in Israelite hands but concerning which no battles at all are recounted. However, we know for a fact that pre-conquest Canaan was hurting and hurting bad from taxations, conscriptions, and all such government squeezes on the part of the local city-state kings and their Egyptian overlords. There would be every reason to believe that the place was full of *'apiru* and those on the verge of going that way, people at the limit of social and economic subsistence and those who had slipped over it into "volunteer" slavery.

In this situation came Joshua and his little band. They had not the manpower to face down Canaanite armies in open conflict; they had not (as we romantically idealize) superbrilliant strategies born out of experience in the desert;

[2] "The Hebrew Conquest of Palestine," *The Biblical Archaeologist*, Vol. XXV, No. 3, September 1962, pp. 66ff.

they had no weapons to speak of (Canaanites knew the manufacture of iron; the Israelites did not); and (if we may express an opinion) they had not powerful religious magic to dissolve city walls and make the sun stand still. No, but what they did have was a *gospel,* a proclamation of good news. And there is nothing quite so powerful as a real, true gospel.

"Yahweh, God of all the earth, is for *Hebrews!*" the announcement read. Or, "He who has no money, come, buy and eat"; or, "Come to me, all who labor and are heavy-laden, and I will give you rest"—to cite later renderings. At this word, Mendenhall suggests, the phenomenon which we already have noted with Jonathan and the Philistines went into effect. Canaanite *'apiru* came swarming out of the ground (into which their overlords had pressed them) to become *'ibri,* followers of Yahweh the *'ibri* God; and Canaan was conquered (and this precisely by the power of God, as the Joshua author was intent to declare, although by the power of his gospel rather than his magic).

It would seem to be the case that in some cities enough of the inhabitants turned rebel that with their help Joshua was able to win a military victory. In others, apparently, the population came over so completely as to make battle unnecessary—thus accounting for the blank areas in the Joshua account. And there were, of course, some cities and areas which simply were not taken.

But don't be too sure that we have not here also stumbled onto the mode of God's final, eschatological conquest. Not, of course, that the poor are going to rise up and smash their oppressors—that is too contradictory to the Lamb's War which we already have established as central to that conquest—but that the poor and the outcast, hearing the gospel that Yahweh is God of the Hebrews, may make the difference. After all, Jesus adopted as his own program:

The Spirit of the Lord is upon me,
because he has anointed me to preach good news to the poor.
He has sent me to proclaim release to the captives

and recovering of sight to the blind,
to set at liberty those who are oppressed,
to proclaim the acceptable year of the Lord.

(Luke 4:18–19)

And catch Luke's version of the Beatitudes:

Blessed are you poor, for yours is the kingdom of God.

Blessed are you that hunger now, for you shall be satisfied.

Blessed are you that weep now, for you shall laugh.

Blessed are you when men hate you, and when they exclude you and revile you, and cast out your name as evil, on account of the Son of man! Rejoice in that day, and leap for joy, for behold, your reward is great in heaven; for so their fathers did to the prophets.

But woe to you that are rich, for you have received your consolation.

Woe to you that are full now, for you shall hunger.

Woe to you that laugh now, for you shall mourn and weep.

Woe to you, when all men speak well of you, for so their fathers did to the false prophets.

But I say to you that hear, Love your enemies, do good to those who hate you, bless those who curse you, pray for those who abuse you. To him who strikes you on the cheek, offer the other also; and from him who takes away your cloak do not withhold your coat as well. Give to every one who begs from you; and of him who takes away your goods do not ask them again. And as you wish that men would do to you, do so to them.

(Luke 6:20–31)

And mind you, that last paragraph, the Lamb's War paragraph, is addressed to the poor to whom he just promised that they will come out on top. He incites revolt and then prohibits it. It is obvious, then, is it not, why a God

of eucatastrophic capabilities is necessary if the ethic of
promise is to have any chance of getting off the ground?
But also there is no question, is there, as to the name of
the God whom Jesus represents? And notice how beautifully the poverty of Yahweh's beloved and the defenselessness of the Lamb's followers fit together, like a hand and
glove.

But all this says something to which we jolly well better
give attention. If we white, affluent, top-o'-the-world Ameri-
cans have it in mind to bring *our* Christianity to all the
poor, suffering people and generously share *our* blessings
with them, then we can just come off it. For if God is
who he says he is, and if it be true that the *'ibri* shall inherit
the earth, then if it should turn out that *we* also have a
share with God's people, this is thanks only to the grace of
God—and perhaps also to the honest recognition that, before God, we too are *'ibri* and nothing more.

When you come right down to it, the first command of
the gospel is not so much that we Christians *help* the poor
as it is that we make ourselves poor, that we make ourselves *one with* the poor.

And this leads me to something I wasn't quite ready to
do. Up to this point we have been addressing ourselves to
broad aspects of *social* ethics—war, violence, depersonali-
zation, poverty, race, minority rights. Now we are forced
to shift over into matters of so-called "personal" morality;
but what's the difference? I intended to make the shift in
the next chapter anyway.

What I have in mind for now is to sound off about the
obscenity of *Playboy* magazine. (Don't get your back up.
We aren't even talking about sex—although your reaction
may betray what is on your mind.) I am talking about those
damned ads (that is not profanity but a considered theological judgment). But look at them! As clearly as Madi-
son Avenue expertise can do it, they say, "A man has a
right—indeed, a moral obligation—to as much luxury as

he can afford. It is valid to spend any amount of money on any item as long as it gives pleasure and satisfaction. The only moral shortcoming of modern man is that his tastes are not yet as refined and expensive as they could be; but when he learns to live according to the Playboy Guide, this is the kingdom of heaven."

Of course, *Playboy* is not the particular villain; we are— our whole society is. *Playboy* I can skip; but on New Year's Day when a man is trying to get some honest relaxation from book writing by watching a bit of football on the tube, what does he get but a string of airline commercials which simply assume that the great American public can, should, or should *want to* join the jet set and, in a blast of wine, women, and song, fly off to the pleasure islands of the world—at great expense to themselves (interpret that as you will) and at great profit to the airline. And of course, unless this assumption about the American public were correct, neither the airlines nor their ad agencies would be fishing with such bait.

Seriously, brethren, not war, not violence, not sex, not race, but affluence well may mark the moral crisis that could sink this nation. For how can we follow this line or allow it to be the order of our day and still pretend to have any relationship to the God of the *Hebrews* or claim a part in the kingdom which he has promised to people of a very different stripe? Our chosen route to the kingdom of God can take us only to the devil.

The issue at stake is not our responsibility to the poor— as though picayunish Christmas baskets or even multimillion-dollar poverty programs could satisfy the matter and free us to chase the *Playboy*-airline star. The issue concerns our becoming poor. Jesus advised the rich young ruler to sell all he had, give it to the poor, and come follow; and it is clear that this counsel was directed not so much to the good of the poor as to that of the young man himself. Now it may well be that such counsel is more than any readers (or writers) of this book presently are prepared to undertake; but we should have the grace to indicate that we at least have heard the message and are willing to let it affect our lives in some way or other.

11

It's a Mad, Mad, Mad, Mad Morality

———————

At points that last chapter got heated enough that perhaps we should use this one to cool it. The bit of fluff presented here represents by far and away the most attention-catching piece I ever have written or ever hope to write. And that is a sad state of affairs. It is a far better thing I do now . . .

Following the appearance of "The *MAD* Morality" in *The Christian Century,* there were letters, there were telegrams from publishers, there were radio broadcasts, there were TV shows, there were newspaper articles, there were *Look* magazine pieces, there were fame (notice I did not say "and fortune"). *Sic transit gloria* (i.e., unhealthy transports of glory)—all for the sake of a not very profound and not very consequential observation regarding a not very profound and not very consequential magazine.

But I have consoled myself that more was involved: The enthusiasm generated by "The *MAD* Morality" indicated that I had touched a deep and widely felt (though largely unexpressed) dissatisfaction with the new morality. Perhaps we already have spoken to some aspects of that dissatisfaction, but there is another that deserves attention here.

The new morality, with its "exceptions" and its uneasiness about law, has had the effect (whether deliberate or not) of suggesting that there are many private actions which entail only the person (or couple) involved and which, therefore, do not properly fall under the rubric of "morality." In such cases one is free to play it his own way. "As long as I am not hurting anyone else, I have a right to do what I want."

This view, we contend, reflects a very narrow concept of "morality" and a very narrow understanding of the nature of persons. The eschatological perspective of the ethic of promise can help broaden these out into a more realistic picture.

Christian eschatology, of course, speaks not so much about the private destiny of separated individuals as about the destiny of the race as a whole (not that the individual loses his significance thereby). Eschatology brings with it, then, a sense of community and mutual involvement. If my regard is toward humanity as a whole, then my own humanity is a precious part of it. More particularly, if I am called to be "a man for others"—a phrase which the new morality does better at reciting than applying—I have no more right to squander, dissipate, or endanger my own humanity than I do theirs. A Christian is not his own possession; he belongs to his Lord for the sake of his brethren to the furtherance of the kingdom. Anything I do to myself that keeps me from being the most effective servant possible, or that unnecessarily shortens my term of service, is to steal what belongs to them. If Jesus is the model of "a man for others," the phrase can imply nothing different.

So any action that has an effect on human welfare is a "moral issue"; and—you're right—very little happens in the world of men that does not involve morality; and because my welfare is part and parcel with human welfare, there is no sector left in which I can do as I please without regard to society.

This much, at least, the *MAD* morality understands; and this, I believe, is one reason why the article hit a responsive chord with the reading public: It gives the lie to the suggestion that here is a personal sphere in which my actions do not affect others. And so, by popular demand (both my wife and I thought it would be nice) we now bring back:

The *MAD* Morality: An Exposé

[PUBLISHER'S NOTE: All of the Editor's Notes and other ridiculous touches found herein are the property of *The Christian Century* and do in no sense originate with or refer to Doubleday & Company.]

The Caesars of contextual ethics have told us that morality, like all gall, is divided into three parts: (1) the authoritarian legalists take the high road (too high); (2) the lawless libertarians take the low (too low); and (3) in between, on the smogless plain, the new morality moves purposefully back and forth.

Obviously there is something wrong with this typology. It is clear that the ethical theory regnant in respectable circles even before the new morality put in its appearance hardly could have been classified under either (1) or (2). Neither the Niebuhr brothers nor Paul Ramsey could have been called legalists or libertarians, so they must have been new moralists; yet it also is clear that the new morality is intended to be something actually new and different from theirs. There just must be more than the three simple options.

My purpose is to present one: the *MAD* Morality. Now because the very fact that the present company is reading *The Christian Century* is proof enough that they aren't quite "with it," I must explain that *MAD* denotes a magazine. It is a periodical of about the same size and heft as the *Century* and printed on the same sort of shoddy paper. Both sell for 30 cents cheap and the *Century*'s is a donation to a non-profit foundation. The important difference, however, is that *MAD* has pictures and is funny. Granted, the *Century* rates as high as the next one in being a funny magazine, but in its case the word has a slightly different connotation.

[NOTE: Eller should know that we are publishing his article for the same reason, and only for the reason, that

MAD publishes its garbage—in the hope that it will help sell at least a few extra copies.—ED.]

Whether the *MAD* morality should be described as an old morality or a new morality is rather hard to say; essentially it is old morality in a new form—old-fashioned morality but without mora*lism*. A distinction must be made between "morality" and "moralism." A "morality" refers to the *content* of ethical teaching, what it affirms as being right and condemns as being wrong; "moralism" denotes a means, a style, by which morality is taught and enforced: a handing down of edicts in an arbitrary, authoritarian, no-nonsense sort of way—regardless of whether the edicts be right or wrong, good or bad.

Evident though it is that modern society is in a moral crisis, the trouble has come not so much because of the old moral standards as because of the moralistic way in which those standards have been presented. The new morality has reacted against this moralism by striving to adapt and modify the moral standard itself—a case of *not* throwing the baby out with her bath . . . if she is old enough to make the gatefold of *Playboy* magazine. But the new morality is no answer, premised as it is upon a too flattering, unrealistic anthropology which assumes that average people (even the kids—who are anything but "average") are smart enough, informed enough, good enough, and well intentioned enough that the simple admonition "Always respect the personality of your brother (or sister)" is sufficient to bring one through even the glandular crisis of a parked car.

The *MAD* morality is of a vastly different stripe. The moral code reflected in the pages of *MAD* is strait-laced enough to put to shame any Sunday school paper in the land. *MAD* takes out after alcohol, tobacco, drugs, licentiousness, deceit, hypocrisy, et al. with a brash and blatant zeal that in comparison makes Billy Sunday sound as tolerant as Joseph Fletcher if not Hugh Hefner. Nor does it overlook the issues of social morality. Judged strictly by the evils it speaks out against, *MAD* represents as old-fashioned a morality as currently is in circulation.

Besides, the *MAD* morality is based upon the old, realistic, biblical anthropology. In fact, the magazine is dedicated to the proposition that the human animal is at base a rather stupid and hypocritical clod. Although Christ may be the model of what we are to *become, MAD* knows that the type of what we *are* is Alfred E. Neuman, that we are not the little Jesuses the new morality takes us for—not even our dear young people. Whereas the Christian world tends to read the hippies and their brethren as embodying the righteous protest of the innocent against the moral hypocrisy of their perverted elders, *MAD,* though not for a moment denying the justice of such a protest, has been particularly effective in making the point that in their way the protestors are just as hypocritical as the aged establishment is in its. Thus, while presentations of the new morality inevitably close with the benediction "God bless all you lovely people in your lovely efforts at finding new and astonishing ways of expressing LUV," the benediction closing each feature in *MAD* is "How stupid can you get?" And yet . . . and yet, especially with kids, *MAD* is much more popular than the new morality.

How can this be? It is here that the plot behind the magazine must be exposed. *MAD* is teaching an old, a real old morality—*but without moralism*. The shift was neat but actually very easy: Where the old moralism said "wrong," *MAD* simply reads "stupid." And though "wrong" and "stupid" actually are morally synonymous (an action is morally wrong, and ethics rule against it, when its tendency is to destroy and harm persons; but it comes to the same thing to say that it is stupid for persons to harm and destroy one another), that little switch makes all the difference. In both cases it is the same old morality, but where the old moral*ism* said, "We *tell* you this is wrong, so don't do it!" *MAD* says, "We can *show* you this is stupid,

so decide whether or not you want to be a stupe!" And
moralism the kids rebel against; *MAD* they eat up.

The full truth of the *MAD* morality came to me in a
discussion with a small group of high school kids. It was at
a church camp, and it needs to be said that these young
people belonged to the Church of the Brethren. By tradition the Brethren have taught and held to a rather high
and stringent morality (I have not said "moral*ism*" at this
point). For instance, the church used to advertise itself as
being "the oldest temperance society in America"—a line
not heard too often nowadays. In any case, the historical
evidence indicates that the eighteenth-century Brethren
founders maintained a quite exalted moral standard—without any particular taint of moralism. But in the nineteenth
century the balance slipped, and the Brethren went through
an orgy of oppressive and petrifying legalism. Then, during
the past fifty years or so, the move has been gradually but
decisively away from the authoritarianism of a strict code-
ethic. But because the memory of it has rankled, in at
least some circles of the church the new morality is being
taken to with considerable spontaneous enthusiasm.

I opened the discussion at camp by asking the kids what
they felt about the teaching they had received from the
church regarding personal morality—smoking, drinking,
sex, etc. The immediate reply was that they hated it, re-
sented being preached to and told what to do and what
not to do. A girl named Cheryl said she was sure it would
be better if the church would just keep quiet about such
things.

I expressed some surprise at the vehemence of this response and said that in my view the church was doing a
pretty good job of keeping quiet already. I was familiar
with the youth curriculum (having written part of it myself) and knew very well that matters of personal habit
barely get mentioned there, and then in a way to which
the newest moralist hardly could object. The youth paper

distributed by the Brethren, the same as that used by the Episcopal Church and the United Church of Christ, is such that not even a hippie could fault it on this score.

"Well then," they responded, "this moralism in the church [although by this time they weren't quite sure whether they actually had experienced it or whether they simply were repeating clichés which young people are expected to repeat about the church] must come from the Sunday school teachers themselves rather than from the printed materials."

"In any case," I said, "it strikes me as real funny that you blow up if the church so much as mentions these things; yet when *MAD* opens up on them in a way that no Sunday school teacher would think of doing, you take it and like it."

That stopped them.

Carole was the first to recover; she decided to take the line that "there is nothing serious in *MAD;* it's all just for laughs."

I challenged her and dashed back to the cabin to get my copies. *MAD* I carry with me; the *Century* I read in the library. [NOTE: This shows how 30-cents-cheap Eller is.—ED.]

We started through, page by page. An antismoking ad. An antiliquor ad. A telling demonstration that the new TV shows which the networks bill as being so great we honestly know to be garbage. A satire making the point that most advertising is pure hogwash if not worse. A caustic commentary about the petty falsifying that goes on in our everyday business transactions. A slam against anti-Semitism. A most effective whack at the John Birch Society. One number of *MAD* deals with more moral issues—and takes stronger stands on them—than does a year's total output by most church publishers.

Then we came to a parody of the surfing movies that were then the rage. I quoted to the group the part where She says to Him: "You know why these beach pictures are so popular, Go-Go? Because teen-agers in the audience like to identify with us and all our dancing and making out!" To which He answers Her: "That's right! It takes their minds off the humdrum things in their own lives . . . like dancing and making out!"

I put it to the kids: "Now isn't that a pretty blunt way of saying that if life is to be at all meaningful it's got to consist of something more than just dancing and making out?" To which Carole (the same Carole who not ten minutes before had *insisted* that there is nothing serious in *MAD*) responded: "Yes, but the church never would be that serious and honest with us."

I for one do not believe that young people really accept or want to hear the flattering view of themselves that underlies the new morality. Down deep they know that *MAD* presents a more accurate picture of their own moral character, competence, and concern. The church would do well to take a lesson in honesty from *MAD* rather than to keep on trying to sweet-talk its young people into being good.

"But why," I pressed, "are you so willing and happy to take all this moralizing from *MAD* and yet so resentful if the church tries to say even a word?"

Cheryl came back: "It's because the church always *tells* you, but *MAD* lets you draw your own conclusions!"

Cheryl was only half right, but in that half lies the secret of the *MAD* morality, the secret that enables *MAD* magazine to get away with teaching a thirteenth-century ethic to twentieth-century young people (thirteenth century B.C., that is—like, say, the Ten Commandments). *MAD* lets the kids *think* they are drawing their own conclusion, although the truth is that it already has drawn the picture in such a way that the conclusion is a foregone matter. Actually, *MAD* is every bit as preachy as that old codifier Moses. Beneath the pile of garbage that is *MAD* there beats, I suspect, the heart of a rabbi.

It has been only with deep reluctance that I have brought myself to write this public exposé. The revelation may put an end to the whole crafty game and break up the good thing *MAD* has going. This would be particularly true if word ever got out that a magazine named *The Christian Century* (how stuffy and pretentious can a title get?) was interested in *MAD*. My consolation comes from the knowledge that there aren't all that many influential people (influential with teen-agers, that is) reading the *Century*. And if it should turn out that my little piece excites a few old fuddy-duddies to rush to the nearest newstand (libraries don't carry *MAD*—so much the worse for libraries) and buy a copy in order to check it out, perhaps the *MAD* men will forgive me (they aren't careful about whom they sell to).

[NOTE: Because the *Century* has no intention of taking a back seat to *MAD* when it comes to moral honesty, we must point out that all the editor's notes contained herein (including this one) were written by Eller. Further, if we are going to be really honest, we must voice the suspicion that the whole piece is a ploy to prod *MAD* into following the lead of *Playboy* magazine and hiring a religion editor—and with comparable inducements (though what all inducements the *Playboy* post involves we have no way of knowing). But Eller has grand dreams of becoming the first *MAD* theologian—or at least the first to admit the title. However, the distinction is this: The *Playboy* position requires a theologian without morals. Such, of course, come a dime a dozen. But a *MAD* religion editor would have to be a puritan with a sense of humor, and you don't see that kind very often.—ED.]

(If this thing catches on, it may end up with the *Century*'s acquiring a religion editor. That would be the day! What his qualifications would have to be God only knows. And what the *Century* would offer as inducements, probably not even God knows.—V.E.)

12

Drink to Me—Only With Thine Eyes

———————◆———————

Some time after *The Christian Century* published "The *MAD* Morality" (our Chapter Eleven) they published "The Ethic of Promise" (our Chapter One). And then—wouldn't you know?—less than a month later they come out with some other guy's article that paid no attention whatsoever to all the fine truths I had been proclaiming.[1] (What's the use of talking if even your friends won't listen?)

Evans' argument was that for the church (or such churches as do) to teach total abstinence from alcoholic beverages is a very foolish and even wrong thing. In the first place, it is old hat to be teaching abstinence when 60 per cent of adult Methodists, 70 per cent of the total U.S. population, and an even higher percentage of the college population already are drinking. QUESTION: Since when has what Methodists *are* doing become the norm for what *Christians* ought to do? Even John Wesley wouldn't buy that one. (By the way, I know the answer to my "since when" question: Since the new morality was invented.) But if a moral teaching is not to be taught as long as the mass of society is practicing something different, the New Testament never could have gotten itself written to begin with.

In the second place, for the church to teach total abstinence gives guilt complexes to nice, honest, upright drinkers. COMMENT: Sorry about that! Of course, the church

[1] J. Claude Evans, "A Consensus on Drinking?" (*The Christian Century*, August 28, 1968).

does have a concern regarding guilt feelings and has some counsel to give about how to deal with them. But the throwing away of moral standards so that people won't have to feel guilty about breaking them is hardly the helpful solution—on this principle we could wind up with a bunch of innocent-feeling debauchees.

In the third place, it is confusing for people to discover that some churches teach total abstinence and others do not. OBSERVATION: But there are two routes to ecumenical unanimity: The churches that do not teach abstinence could begin to; why assume that those who do must cease to? The fact that there is this confusion gives absolutely no guidance as to which way it should be resolved.

In the fourth place, Jesus drank. PROPOSAL: If the new moralists will quit dragging in this hoary old irrelevancy, I will try to persuade the WCTU to drop some of theirs. Jesus, also, as he traveled about the country, probably walked in the *middle* of the road—which would be a very stupid thing to try in our day and age. What Jesus in fact *did* is relevant to what *we* should do only if it can be shown that the social problem posed by alcohol in his day was at least to some extent comparable to what it poses in our own. "Contextualism" ought to mean at least this much.

Evans' conclusion is: "Our goal, however, should be a society where there is no pressure to drink if one is an abstainer, and no moral condemnation of acceptable drinking if one is not an abstainer, with the entire culture united in opposition to drunkenness as positively unacceptable." A NON-CONCLUSION: We have not yet begun to fight (in proving Evans' conclusion *wrong*); our interest is simply to show that he has not argued to any conclusion at all. The difficulty is that each step of his argument uses as its *premise* the proposition which he is trying to *prove,* namely that the moderate use of alcoholic beverages entails no moral issue. What his whole article comes to is this: If a person's choice in regard to imbibing is not a moral question, the church should not drag morality into the matter.

Well, obviously! Except that that little "if" deserves some examination and support, of which Evans supplies not a whit.

Such inquiry, it seems logical, would have to include some assessment as to the scope and nature of the alcohol problem in our society. We here make bold to supply what Evans skipped.

The following statistics have been gleaned from a variety of sources; I cannot vouch for their absolute accuracy, and they do not represent an all-out effort to get the very latest and most complete information. Nevertheless, in sum they undoubtedly point toward a true picture of the magnitude and scope of the alcohol problem in the United States today.

The nation spends $13 billion per year on drinks—an expenditure that should raise moral doubts even if the drinks had no aftereffects. However, taking care of the after-effects costs more than the drinks themselves; in one year the state of California spent $62 million *more* in after-costs than it collected in liquor taxes. Through absenteeism, impaired work capability, etc., it is estimated that alcohol misuse costs American industry between $4 and $7.5 billion annually.

We have in our midst some 6.5 million persons whose humanity has grossly degenerated through alcoholism, plus no telling how many others for whom drinking has created serious problems—affecting personality, health, and/or longevity. There seems to be a direct correlation between the high alcoholism rate of certain population centers and their high suicide rate.

Out of arrests of all sorts, 40 per cent are for drunkenness and drunk driving. The director of the crime laboratory of the Columbus (Ohio) police department says: "In our city we know from additional alcohol tests of persons arrested immediately after the commission of a felony that beverage alcohol contributed to at least two thirds of those crimes, and we have reason to believe the percentage is higher—much higher."

At least 50 per cent of fatal highway accidents are caused by drunken drivers.

A Chicago judge is of the opinion that at least 33 per cent of all child delinquency comes about because of drinking parents. Only 28 per cent of children from alcoholic families grow up free from mental or physical damage attributable to the alcoholism.

We haven't figures, but undoubtedly alcohol plays a significant role in family tensions and marital breakups. How many children are deprived because family income is spent on drinks? How many important decisions are muffed by minds fogged with alcohol?

When the facts are faced it is apparent that we here are dealing with a situation which, as regards its pernicious effect on human values, is comparable in seriousness to such situations as the Vietnam war, racial discrimination, poverty, and perhaps even our dehumanizing university systems. If our concern for human welfare justifies our reading these other situations as moral crises which call for radical protest and action, so too this. True moral sensitivity does not take the prerogative of picking and choosing some dehumanizing situations to decry with great passion while conveniently overlooking others that are just as serious. It is, by the way, precisely this selective blindness that makes me just a little leery of the so highly vaunted moral concern of today's youth. But be that as it may, beverage alcohol does pose a king-sized moral problem somewhere along the way.

Claude Evans contends that the problem lies in "drunkenness" rather than in "drinking" as such. How much he would include under drunkenness he does not specify, but it almost would have to include whatever sort of drinking that leads to the effects described above (whether that level can be defined and made practical is another question). His so locating the moral crux is, of course, altogether right and proper—if he can demonstrate that drunkenness in fact can be controlled without involving the question of drinking per se. But this he does not do or even attempt to do.

To cite periods from the past (as he cites Jesus' day) or even subcultures within present American society (as he cites the Jews, the Italians, and the Chinese) is little to the point. The question must be: "Can drunkenness be so controlled *today* in the *dominant U.S. culture?*" (Sometimes there is value in forcing the new morality to be contextualist.) What if it were the case, for example, that the Jews are able to drink and yet avoid drunkenness not simply because they express social disapproval of drunkenness but also because they have the sort of family structure and parental respect that gives that disapproval force? Then all Evans would have to do is get the American family reconstructed before his proposal becomes practical. Does he seriously believe that this approach can be made to work when respect for parents is in sharp decline and social disapproval something the younger generation seems to seek rather than avoid?

His proposal, recall, is that "the entire culture be united in opposition to drunkenness as positively unacceptable." A good idea! It ought to be tried! But the very truth is that this is precisely what is being taught and tried—much more seriously than ever has been the case with abstinence. Consider that all of those churches and individuals who practice abstinence by the same token are opposing drunkenness; that group is in Evans' corner to begin with. In addition, all the rest of the churches (i.e., those that do not disapprove of drinking) certainly oppose and teach against drunkenness. In fact, Evans may have hit upon the one item in regard to which all the churches of the country *are* united —in their opposition to drunkenness.

To greater effect than the churches, Evans has on his side one of the richest lobbies and most powerful propaganda machines that has ever existed—namely the liquor industry. That group has the most deep-seated interest here; drunkenness is bad for their business. Indeed, all the millions of dollars spent in liquor advertising amount to a concerted educational campaign on how to drink acceptably.

Find me one liquor advertisement that so much as hints that drunkenness is a proper use of the product (*MAD* magazine doesn't count).

Almost all of the people represented in the statistics above are opposed to drunkenness. None of them set out to become drunks or are advocating the position now; and their example constitutes a very graphic warning against drunkenness. All of the nation's employers who are hurt by absenteeism are opposed to drunkenness and take steps to discourage it. The schools, civic organizations, the law enforcement agencies, and even the law itself (40 per cent of all arrests) express nothing but disapproval over drunkenness and particularly drunk driving. A majority of college students (I would wager) frown upon drunkenness, and the administrations work actively to suppress it. There probably are very few homes in which the drunkenness of the children is "laughed at or shrugged off" (as Evans put it).

How much more could he realistically expect than he is getting already? His program has been and is being tried on a rather grand scale. A recent study, *Teen-age Drinking,* by Margaret Bacon and Mary Brush Jones (Crowell, 1968), would indicate that the great majority of teen-agers already are drinking for what Evans would call the right reasons and in the right way, i.e., with their parents' permission, introduced to the practice at home and without being made to feel guilty. And a *Time* magazine editorial-essay concluded: ". . . With more drinking but less drunkenness, the U.S. stands established as a moderate drinking society, in which social custom is beginning to serve as a far better control over the drinking habit than either statutes or disapproval."

Let us be very honest about what those who take this sort of a position are saying. Namely: The American public is not enough concerned about the social damage indicated by our statistics to take any action as drastic as giving up their booze. In effect they have chosen, rather, to tolerate and live with the problem *essentially as it is*. (There is no indication that there is a great deal more that can be done in the way of education toward proper drinking and no evidence that such efforts would mark any real change in the alcohol picture.)

Indeed, the nature of the case makes one suspect rather strongly that, given the character of our society, there is something about alcohol itself that tends to lead many users from drinking to drunkenness *in spite of any and all social disapproval that might be exerted* and often in spite of the individual's own intention. Of course, it must be admitted that the teaching of total abstinence has not solved the liquor problem either; but this can be said: Almost all of the unhappy people represented in our statistics come out of the ranks of Evans' party—i.e., they began with "acceptable drinking," were opposed to drunkenness, and had every intention of keeping it that way. On the other hand, no total abstainer ever has gotten drunk.

Yet Evans' reading of the situation undoubtedly is the realistic one. Under a Niebuhrian sort of concern for what is pragmatic and prudential, the only counsel that makes sense is to try to minimize the damage and make it as tolerable as possible *within the limits of a drinking society*. It is futile and irrelevant to demand abstinence or push for prohibition, and to do so has the effect only of making well-intentioned drinkers feel guilty. (QUESTION: Is protest against war any less futile and irrelevant? And is Evans as concerned about the guilty conscience that such protests create among well-intentioned war makers?)

Society, then, will drink and will have to do the best it can in living with the consequences. But Christians don't have to go along with such defeatism; they have heard the promise of the kingdom. And such a consideration opens up the alternative that Evans has not glimpsed. Throughout his article he speaks now to the church and now to society —never once considering that different moral standards might apply to the two groups. He does not think in terms of a "Christian" morality. It may be that what Evans proposes is as much as ever can be expected from the world. Society is too attached to its booze, would rather suffer this major human blight than sacrifice its liquid enjoyment. It may be that total abstinence will have to be an arcane discipline within the Christian community.

And yet the case here is not quite parallel with that of the non-resistance which we discussed earlier. To ask the world (the world which has not heard the promise of the kingdom) to give up its military establishments is, from its frame of reference, to ask it to give up national freedom and even the means of survival. To give up liquor, on the other hand, is to give up only a luxury item which in no way is necessary to human well-being or even happiness. It should be possible to make a case for abstinence to a secular humanist as well as to the Christian.

And now for the case: Love *is* what God *does;* and what God does is, by bringing men under his kingly rule, advance humanity as a whole toward the kingdom of God. Human love, therefore, is to co-operate with God in the achievement of this end. God is "the God for others" (with a bias toward the "Hebrews" who need him most); and the Christian must be "a man for others" (with the same bias— and in this case particularly toward those "Hebrews" who constitute or who are destined to constitute the alcohol statistics above). Our pitch will center not so much on what drinking may or may not do to *me* (i.e., the hypothetical "me" who is as much you as he is me) as on what will be the most loving service I can perform for "the weaker brethren."

Our argument, then, will not be "Whoever takes a drink is damned to hell." (In that regard, the new morality often tries to strengthen its case by setting up straw men, namely the old-fashioned moralisms that hardly are current anywhere and certainly not among any audience the new moralists can hope to command.) Indeed, those who would counter this argument often fall into the trap of accepting its premises. How often have I heard college kids—intelligent, well-meaning college kids—say: "Oh, I grant you that drinking [or more often, smoking] is harmful, but it isn't a *moral* question." Now I haven't the slightest idea what "moral" possibly might mean in such a case. Rather, I do know but can't believe that any thinking person would buy such superstitious theology. *Moral* questions, now, assume that somewhere God has set up a bunch of completely arbitrary laws that have no relation to what actually helps or harms man and that, when a person breaks one of these, God sends him some sort of supernatural punishment quite independent of the natural consequences of the act.

If this is what moral questions are, then I don't believe that there are *any* moral questions. But what I do believe is that wherever people are being hurt unnecessarily, wherever men are being deprived of the full humanity that God desires for them, there—by definition—is a *moral* question.

Obviously, the superstitious definition of "moral" assumes a very strong concept of *prescriptive* law (God has set up an edict and will call to account anyone who so much as questions it), smacks of authoritarianism, and is as legalistic as all get out. Our approach to the alcohol problem wants nothing to do with all this—although it does not follow that alcohol becomes any less a concern (and a deeply *moral* concern). However, from the standpoint of law as *descriptive,* it seems evident (at least to me) that the kingdom goal would have to be described as society without an alcohol problem. Abstinence seems to be the only strategy that shows any promise of getting us there. And it would seem entirely proper, then, that the church challenge, exhort, educate, and encourage its members to abstain from drink. Inevitably this will bring a degree of disapproval upon members who choose to do otherwise; but the church's discipline here, as in all other cases, must represent the community's loving effort to help a brother voluntarily accept the discipline of God and not be simply an act of condemnation.

Why, then, should a Christian abstain from alcoholic beverages? The first, though not decisive, consideration is that, by becoming a drinker, he may drift into our statistics and so impair his own ability to serve humanity. Of course, no Christian who chooses to drink intends that this should happen, and he is confident that he is capable of keeping it from happening to him. Yet it does happen, and even to the best of Christians; sincere and committed church leaders inadvertently have wound up as part of the problem. Statistically the risk may not be very high; the damage, however, can be of tragic proportions (even if it were only one unnecessary death on the highway, one career ruined, one vital decision missed because of a befogged mind); and the risk is so easy to eliminate entirely.

Yet, for the sake of the argument, let us assume that I am as strong and competent as I think I am (still speaking, of course, of the hypothetical "I" who is as much you as he is me), that I am one of the majority who can drink without adverse consequences. This still is not the end of the matter. The Bible speaks directly to our next consideration—and that with much more relevance than passages about the drinking of Jesus or Paul's advising Timothy to take a little wine "for the stomach's sake."

What follows is 1 Corinthians 8, modified by the insertion of some new words (printed in italics). In many cases we simply substitute "moral competence" where Paul had "knowledge." The Corinthian Christians to whom Paul was writing were confident that they possessed a superior knowledge which made them exceptional —and do not proponents of the new morality show a similar confidence in their "moral competence"? We should like to be shown where our modified version changes Paul's point in the slightest or is any less relevant to the alcohol problem than his was to the problem of food offered to idols.

Now concerning *alcoholic beverages:* we know that "all of us possess *moral competence.*" "*Moral competence*" puffs up, but love builds up. If any one imagines that he *is morally competent,* he does not yet know as he ought to know. But if one loves God, one is *given moral guidance* by him.

Hence, as to the *drinking of alcohol,* we know that "*one drink never hurt anybody,*" and that "*if people would learn to drink properly they wouldn't get into trouble. . . .*"

However, not all possess this knowledge. But some, *because of their make-up or situation, drink to excess;* and their *moral competence,* being weak, is defiled. *Booze* will not commend us to God. We are no worse off if we do not *drink,* and no better off if we do. Only take care lest this liberty of yours somehow become a stumbling block to the weak. For if any one sees you, a man of *moral competence,* at table *with a glass,* might he not be encouraged, if his *competence* is weak, to *drink to excess?* And so by your *moral competence* this weak man is destroyed, the brother for whom Christ died. Thus sinning against your brethren and wounding their *moral competence* when it is weak, you sin against Christ. Therefore, if *drink* is a cause of my brother's falling, I will never *drink,* lest I cause my brother to fall.

Yet even if I were to discount the risk of my own slipping, and if I were to take every precaution (such as drinking in secrecy) against causing my brother (including my own children) to fall, there would seem still to be a consideration that would command abstinence. If I have heard the promise of the kingdom, if I believe that God even now is mightily at work bringing that kingdom to consummation, if it seems clear that the coming of that kingdom necessarily will involve the elimination of all forms of drunkenness, if the evidence is that abstinence is the one effective way to insure against drunkenness, and if the kingdom also promises a quality of happiness that does not need the help of alcohol, then does it not make sense that my volunteering to abstain now can be an aspect of my coming under the present rule of God, a public testimony of my faith in the kingdom promise, a forecast pointing and challenging the world toward that kingdom?

Governor (now U. S. Senator) Harold Hughes of Iowa said something that can be used to lead us to the heart of the matter. Governor Hughes, an active Methodist layman, grew up in an abstinent home but, at college, took to drinking and turned out to be an alcoholic. As he put it, "To me, to drink was to die." He was saved by becoming a teetotaler. Consequently some people were surprised when, as governor, he approved legislation that changed Iowa from a dry state to a wet. In response Governor Hughes said, "If I could do away with liquor by pulling a switch, I certainly would do it. But I can't."[2]

This is a consistent position. Neither the governor of the state nor anyone else has the right to force his moral standards onto the public. Prohibition is desirable only when it is supported by a strong consensus of the people. The best that can be done is to disapprove drunkenness and attempt to control it. There is no switch to pull that will make the kingdom of God come. Yet each Christian does have an obligation to pull as much of switch as he does control, namely his own part in the kingdom and as much influence as he can carry with his brethren.

We have spent an entire chapter on the matter of alcohol, but it should save us from having to write some other chapters. The argument can be applied virtually without change to the problems of tobacco, dope, misuse of prescription drugs, and so on down the line. With very little change (*abstention,* of course, cannot be the norm) it

[2] *Christianity Today* (January 31, 1969), p. 40.

applies to such things as overeating, overwork, lack of exercise, lack of sleep—all these are *moral* problems which rightly are concerns of the Christian faith and thus the Christian community. No man lives to himself; he commands no purely private sector. What he does with *his* humanity affects his contribution to the humanity which God is claiming for his kingdom. Morality is as broad as humanity itself and as focused as the personal actions of any individual within it.

13
The Problem of Religious Language

———◆———

This chapter serves a particular purpose, because in our day no book is worth its theological salt unless it deals with the all-important matter of religious language. The only trouble is that what we are going to talk about is not what theologians have in mind as *the* problem; and what we have in mind bothers them not at all. Nevertheless we have managed to include a chapter entitled "The Problem of Religious Language."

We do not claim now to be discussing a major moral issue that rates the sort of concern deserved by those treated earlier. In fact, our intent is quite different. One effect of the new morality has been to demonstrate (or to claim to have demonstrated) that many issues once considered to be moral are not moral at all; one is free to deal with them as he will. Our hope is that the ethic of promise will work quite the reverse. As men become more aware of the human possibilities involved in the promise of the kingdom, inevitably it will make them more sensitive to those aspects of our life together which fall short of what they could be. Any situation that stifles humanity's move toward the kingdom is, in our definition, a "moral issue"; and the Christian should be glad to discover these, because they then represent an opportunity for correction, improvement, and thus a deeper quality of humanity.

Because they hold such differing concepts of freedom

—as we saw in an earlier chapter—a great psychological divergency comes between the new morality and the ethic of promise at this point. Basically, the new morality sees moral requirements as being oppressive and wants to minimize them so that man can be "free" to follow his inclinations. So the *only* rule is love; love is essentially a good man following his inclinations; and we are all more or less good men, or could be if we would. But under the ethic of promise moral guidance is welcomed as marking the way to the kingdom, the locus of humanity's true freedom, God's kingly rule being the only relationship in which any individual can be truly free. The discovery of moral issues, then, marks not the multiplication of restrictions but invitations toward freedom.

By way of example we shall point up a moral issue of which even the church has shown little awareness —and I probably would not be aware of it myself except that I happen to come out of a religious tradition that has made a point of giving rather close attention to the moral teachings of the New Testament. The issue is oath-swearing.

"Oath-swearing" does not refer to the modern phenomenon of profanity, a problem to which the Bible does not speak—probably indicating that it did not exist in that day. But because it is not our intent to speak about profanity, let us say a word in passing so that it will not feel neglected. After all, one sin has got as many rights as another in this book.

Stop to think about it, and it is just plain weird that some of the most precious words in the language, some that involve the most meaningful and exalted connotations, also should be used in the most careless way imaginable, as thoughtless expressions of anger, frustration, vilification. How did the name that is above every name —that at the name of Jesus every knee should bow—also become the name to express some of the lowest of man's feelings, used when man bows not in reverence but in brutishness? And how can it happen—as I am sure it often does—that one and the same person can use the name both ways?

I think it obvious that, in by far the majority of cases when these highest words are used in the lowest way, there is no real intent to blaspheme or to mock the faith. The usage reflects mere thoughtlessness, a cheapening and vulgarizing of language and man's high privilege of verbal communication. Yet even at this level the matter is one of moral concern—although not an excuse for a rebuttal full of prescriptive fulminations about damnation and hell-fire which mark an equally thoughtless and vulgarizing tendency at the other end of the spectrum. Nevertheless, *thoughtlessness* is a propensity that does great damage to human relations and social well-being, and one that the promise of the kingdom challenges us to eliminate.

But although this vulgar language now represents only carelessness, the question remains as to how the language's holiest terms got chosen for this purpose. Were the words first used in solemn religious oaths and then oath-taking itself demeaned until it was used on each and every occasion? Perhaps so, but my guess is that it was different. It seems likely to me that in the first instance the words were chosen deliberately to hurt and offend the person to whom they were addressed. I can show scorn for another person by using the words which he holds sacred in a scornful manner. I can smear him by smearing his holy things. I can show my superiority over him by trampling upon that to which he bows. And this, of course, speaks of an entirely different order of morality, one that hardly can be excused under any definition of love, that surely must stand in direct contradiction to love.

We have admitted that most of the profanity that is heard does not represent such intent; but no matter how some of our swear words got chosen, it is quite evident that this more vicious use of language is happening among us today—and as often as not on the part of the so-called *"love* children." Toward what freedom was Berkeley's free speech movement actually aimed: the freedom to show people what you think of them by verbally crapping on them (excuse the language, but it has to be strong to do justice to the case).

Much of this free-swinging language—and the free-swinging activity that is part of the same picture—is performed most blithesomely. The stage show *Hair,* the American tribal love rock musical which celebrates capital L-O-V-E love, is the classic example. And the language and activity are defended precisely on the basis of their style. Free, spontaneous, innocent, open, uninhibited are the adjectives used to prove the morality of what goes on (or comes off). Well, maybe . . . but I think of another situation which could rate the same adjectives. A carload of smart-alec high school boys come wheeling past a motorist who is driving too slow for their tastes. As they go past, one of the kids sticks his arm out the window and gives the motorist "the finger." The whole gang laughs like mad.

Free, spontaneous, innocent, open, uninhibited? Perhaps so, but also impatient, unkind, arrogant, rude, irritable, insisting on their own way—almost all the things that Paul says love is not. The justification, of course, is that people need to be shocked out of their hang-ups—if this is the way hang-ups get unhung. Even so, where these people derive their status as moral authorities remains something of a mystery.

Yet it is true that Jesus did plenty of shocking in his day—and used some rather strong language in the process. "Woe to you, hypocrites, you serpents, you brood of vipers." But there is a difference. Jesus used shock in the service of love (i.e., in helping men accept the kingly rule of God) and in himself displayed the qualifications of a true moral authority. His shockers always specified something to be corrected, showed the person a path to a better life, were intended to open ears so that they could hear the promise of the kingdom. But what do most of our modern shockers display? Contempt for squares, arrogant superiority over those who choose to read love and freedom in terms other than *Hair*'s. So if what *Hair* demonstrates is freedom, I'll take the slavery of Christianity. If *Hair* defines love, I feel complimented by its hate. And for the shocks I need, I'll go to Jesus every time, thank you!

And what shall we say of those whose love for their brothers of Vietnam lead them to scream "Murderer! Butcher! Pig!" and Worse! in the faces of other brothers for whom Christ also died? In truth, love is a many-slandered thing. We do face a problem of religious language and one that may be more serious than the one about which the theologians do so much theologizing.

Although it may not have sounded like it, the above was an aside, a passing nod on the way toward getting to another matter—one we would much rather talk about—oath-swearing.

The New Testament speaks very clearly on the matter. In the Sermon on the Mount, Jesus says:

> Do not swear at all, either by heaven, for it is the throne of God, or by the earth, for it is his footstool, or by Jerusalem, for it is the city of the great King. And do not swear by your head, for you cannot make one hair white or black. Let what you say be simply "Yes" or "No"; anything more than this comes from evil.
>
> (Matthew 5:34–37)

James 5:12 picks up almost the same words; and again in Matthew (23:16–22), Jesus takes the scribes and Pharisees to task for the hypocrisy of their oaths.

But although the New Testament speaks so, we have proceeded to make oath-taking an inherent feature of our legal practice without even pausing to ask what Jesus may

have had in mind and whether his concern is legitimate
and relevant. Let us pause for at least the time required to
read a few pages.

The issue at stake is that of personal integrity. Clearly,
the order that God has in mind for society will come
only when all human dealings and relationships are rooted
in strict integrity; this is a major concomitant of the promise of the kingdom. How, then, do religious oaths relate
to integrity?

In the first place, there is the question of integrity
toward God himself. What does it say about the nation's
respect and reverence for God when thousands of times
daily the state administers oaths in the name of God—
without ever making the slightest inquiry as to whether
either the swearer of the oath or its administrator even
believe in God? As clear as day, what we have here is not
the state's desire to submit itself to God but to *use* him
for its own purposes. In fact, the state doesn't even care
whether there *is* a God; all it requires is a name with
which to impress poor sinners. And for that matter, where
does the *secular* state get the authority to administer *religious* oaths? This is a more flagrant violation of the
separation of church and state than any that has exercised
our country up until this time. It would be very interesting
to have someone make a test case of the matter and see
what the Supreme Court could come up with as justification for the practice.

In the second place, what sort of theology lies behind
the use of the oath? Medieval superstition, that's what!
The implication is that if one recites a magic formula
with hand upraised, then automatically God has to pay
attention in a way he does not necessarily do regarding
everyday conversation; and that if after a man has sworn
he proceeds to lie, God is under some special obligation
to knock him to kingdom come (where did that phrase
arise?—it says the very opposite of what we use it to
say). Oath-swearing represents man's baldest sort of at-

tempt to make God into a bottled genie used to serve his own petty purposes. In this case the state enlists God as its official bogeyman to scare the peasantry into shaping up. Although, as Jesus saw, the whole bit is blasphemous, it used to work; now, since the peasantry has come of age, it doesn't even do that, but we keep going through the motions anyhow.

In the third place, what evidence is there that the formality of an oath accomplishes anything at all in preventing liars from lying or in helping honest men to tell the truth? All in the world the state wants or requires is that the witness know that he is liable to perjury. For this, there is no reason to drag God into the matter; a simple declaration by the judge would do as well. If the state wants the truth, let it go after it in its own way. God will get his truth in his way—which has nothing to do with oaths but with winning men into a relationship of personal commitment (including commitment to integrity) and helping them to live out that commitment.

Finally, in the fourth place, the very nature of oaths says something false about the character of Christian integrity. The oath implies that one's responsibility to speak the truth holds only at such times as one is under oath (or at least that his responsibility is greater at such times). Not so, the Christian must insist; his responsibility to speak the truth is continuous and absolute, because it roots in his submission to the kingly rule of God and is empowered and enabled through that rule. By taking the oath and so allowing this other implication to stand, the Christian is betraying his real position.

After a pause for consideration, Jesus' "Swear not at all" turns out to be dealing with a real moral issue rather than a first-century irrelevancy. And it should be known that here is a law of love that can be obeyed, a witness to the kingdom that can be made, without particular risk or inconvenience; the battle already has been fought. Back at the time this country was founded, the same New Testament radicals who were protesting war and slavery (namely the Friends, Brethren, and Mennonites) also protested oath-swearing—and won a concession from the government. It is now the law of the land that, wherever in court situations or legal documents an oath is requested, a person may choose to "affirm" rather than "swear"; that is, he may follow Jesus' counsel and simply give his "yes" to the fact that he is endeavoring to tell the truth rather than going through the fiction that a holy formula in any way effects integrity.

Mention ought also be made of another sort of oath and—wouldn't you know—another sort of difficulty it brings with it. All public school teachers in my part of the country are required as one of their terms of employment to sign the following.[1]

[State of California oath:] I solemnly swear (or affirm) that I will support the *Constitution of the United States of America,* the *Constitution of the State of California,* and the laws of the United States and the State of California and will, by precept and example, promote respect for the Flag and the statutes of the United States and of the State of California, reverence for law and order, and undivided allegiance to the Government of the United States of America.

[County of Los Angeles oath:] I, _____, do solemnly swear (or affirm) that I will support and defend the *Constitution of the United States* and the *Constitution of the State of California* against all enemies foreign and domestic; that I will bear true faith and allegiance to the *Constitution of the United States* and the *Constitution of the State of California;* that I take this obli-

[1] Since this book was written, the California loyalty oath for public schools teachers has come under review by the state Department of Education. It may have been dropped by now.

gation freely without any mental reservation or purpose of evasion; and that I will well and faithfully discharge the duties upon which I am about to enter.

Quite apart from the question as to whether these oaths are of any earthly good in deterring those whom they are designed to deter, we raise the question of their heavenly evil. Jesus put it as a fundamental principle that his followers are to "render unto Caesar the things that are Caesar's and unto God the things that are God's." But in these oaths Caesar seems to take first dubs—without there being much of anything left over that God could claim as his. The assumption would seem to be either that the state *is* God or that one can rest assured "freely without any mental reservation" that the claims of God always will be in perfect accord with those of the United States of America and the state of California. These oaths leave absolutely no room for the possibility that a man might ever have to choose *between* God and the state—although history is replete with instances in which men of Christian conscience have had to make precisely such a choice (and that even in the United States of America, I am sorry to say).

But just how—I leave the question with you—is a Christian to square his radical commitment unto God of the things that are God's with:

·*"reverence* for law and order" as political authorities may choose to define law and order—if "reverence" can properly have law and order as its object in any case;

·*"undivided* allegiance" to a finite and fallible institution of the variety that has had a long history of descents into demonism;

·"defend against *all* enemies" when it could happen, as it happened to God's chosen nation, that God himself becomes the enemy—as a number of the prophets testify;

·"bear *true faith* and *allegiance* to"—the object of that exalted language being two human documents, political in character, secular in origin, changeable and changing, of the world that is passing away as is Caesar and all that is his.

It likely is true that the legislators got carried away, trying to buttress the poverty of their oath's effectiveness by the extravagance of its language, and that there is here no intention of robbing God of his prerogatives. But what happens to Christian integrity when one declares that he is signing "without mental reservation" when in fact he has mental *and spiritual* reservations of a grave order?

14
And Now—Sex!

———————◆◆◆———————

I suppose it is something of a miracle that we have done the better part of a book on morality without mentioning sex, but we can evade the subject no longer.

For my part, I would be happy to forget it. A major factor in today's sex situation is that there is so gosh-awful much talk and attention given to the subject. Just as a rosebush will not grow as it should if someone always is digging it up to see how the roots are doing, so, if our society were healthy, sex could do better with less attention. But as long as the mass media insist on publicizing, displaying, and analyzing sex all over the place, I guess the moralists are obliged to give attention to the matter also—if for no other reason than to try to get the roots back in the ground where they belong.

Rather than beginning straight out with sex proper (or improper), we will lead up to the subject by talking about nudity. The two are not necessarily synonymous—although there does seem to be evidence that the one at times encourages the other.

The little piece that follows originally appeared in one of the small-type back sections of *The Christian Century*. It is, however, something I prize rather highly, because it brought a personal, handwritten note of appreciation from the late editor-in-chief of the *Century*, Kyle Haselden.

I must apologize that the article is so dated as to in-

clude an analysis of *Who's Afraid of Virginia Woolf?*—
particularly since one of Elizabeth Taylor's subsequent
movies is advertised with the catch line: "Makes *Virginia
Woolf* look like *Little Women!*" I may be a prude, but not
so much so that I want to be caught criticizing *Little
Women.* However, there may be an advantage here: If I
can make my point regarding *Virginia Woolf,* then it
should be positively easy to make it cover most of the
stuff that has come out since.

My treatment of *Virginia Woolf* also presents another
little difficulty which ultimately may prove to be an advantage. If Albee's play is an example of the new morality, it
demonstrates on just how different a wave length the
ethic of promise is operating. Albee is quoted as saying
of his major character: "I like Martha. I think she's a
sympathetic character, a pretty good well-rounded woman."[1]
Now either Albee wrote a different play than the one I
read—or else he here uses "well-rounded" in a more literal
sense than that with which moral discourse should concern itself.

THE NUDE MORALITY, OR,
BUT, FELLOWS, WE DON'T LIVE IN EDEN
ANY MORE!

Recognition is due the fact that the fight for the new
morality is being carried on bravely on one front by a
particularly dedicated band of film critics—such men as
Dave Pomeroy (*International Journal of Religious Education* and elsewhere), Lucio P. Ruotolo (*Christianity and
Crisis*), Al Carmines (*Motive*). A notable example of
their work is Clifford Edwards' review in the November
1966 *Motive.* But perhaps the best summary of the position is to be found in Malcolm Boyd's article "Which
Are the Moral Films of Hollywood?" in the Los Angeles
Times, Calendar section, for February 26, 1967.

Boyd says nothing new or exceptional. But he does
list the films which appear to him and to critics of a

[1] Los Angeles *Times, Calendar* section, May 14, 1967, p. 20.

similar ilk to be making "honest and significant moral statements": *Who's Afraid of Virginia Woolf?* (inevitably something of a test case for this point of view), *Darling, The Pawnbroker, Blow-Up, Georgy Girl,* and *Alfie.* And it was while reading Boyd that I was struck by the fact that the great defect of contemporary contextualism is that it ignores precisely what is most fundamental to our human context.

The key concept at stake here is nudity or, more accurately, the process of getting that way, "stripping to the buff" (as it is being heralded Miss Taylor is pleased to do for us in her next picture). Because it can help me say what I want to say, I will use the "stripping" image throughout the following comments. But the reader must keep in mind that I am not thinking exclusively or even predominantly of the mere physical act of taking off one's clothes. The nude morality is much more interested in people who strip themselves bare psychologically, spiritually, humanly. Thus although our topic includes sex, it goes far beyond it.

What Boyd's summary makes quite clear is that the value most highly prized by the new moralists is nudity— being open, honest, frank, bare. Conversely, the sin most detested by them is "piety"—whatever smacks of (or whatever they can interpret as smacking of) cover-up, façade, sham. Apparently it would not be going too far to suggest that for many of them nudity is redemption or, better, that stripping is the way to salvation.

My thesis is that, although there is a valid connection between nudity and redemption, these critics have overlooked the matter of context. There are two situations in which nudity is right and moral. The first is innocence. Clothing was unnecessary and would have been out of place in Eden, as the biblical author well understood. When man was true man, man as God created and intended him, nude was the way he could, should, and did stand before God and his fellows.

But after man corrupted and falsified himself by perverting his God relationship, he felt a need for clothes.
Interestingly enough, God confirmed this judgment: "And
the Lord God made for Adam and for his wife garments
of skins and clothed them." The nudity appropriate to
Eden is not appropriate east of Eden. And we dare not
forget that our present context is outside Paradise, from
which place we are barred until, through his grace, God
restores us to innocence.

Nudity outside Eden signifies something different from
nudity in Eden—which leads us to the second context
within which nudity is right. This is at the spot where
we come closest to our lost innocence, namely "before
God." The Bible describes (and approves) several awe-
some scenes in which men strip themselves utterly naked
before God. Moses is so bold as to complain that he
would rather be murdered by God than carry out the
assignment given him by God; yet God says there is no
one like his servant Moses with whom he speaks face to
face. Job curses God in *Woolf*-type language; yet God
tells Job's friends that they have not spoken of him what
is right, as has his servant Job. Jeremiah accuses God of
having deceived him and made him a laughingstock; yet
God sets him over nations and over kingdoms to destroy
and to overthrow, to build and to plant. Jesus screams,
"My God, my God, why hast thou forsaken me?"; yet
"truly this man was the Son of God." These were men who
stripped to the buff before God. As Martin Buber put it
well: ". . . If only man truly speaks to God, there is
nothing he may not say to him."

But for man to strip before man, a sinner stripping
before a sinner—this is a situation of another sort, a context that points toward another ethic. With God there is
no possibility that the stripping might be motivated by
and used for unworthy ends. Let anyone strip as he will—
whether he be the exhibitionist jailed as a pervert or the
one Hugh Hefner publishes as a gatefold—there is little

chance that he can impress, shock, titillate, or entice God. And don't try to say that the so-called moral films are above these things. It must be recognized that there is an exhibitionism of the psyche as well as of the body, of what is depraved as well as of what is alluring. The advertising and promotion that surround *Woolf, Darling,* et al. make their pitch toward that within us which is farthest from Eden. Most movie-goers attend out of this sort of curiosity, and most of them get what they pay for.

To strip before God is different in still another way. With God there is a second step, the possibility of true redemption. All who strip before God come away new men. But with sinner nude before sinner, what's to be done? Either they can go to bed together (enjoy their nudity for what it is worth as an end in itself) or they can put their clothes back on and go home (nothing changed).

Again, in the context of these "moral" films no stripping deserves the name unless it exposes a filth-encrusted rump. Now the Bible knows all about the dirty bottoms of men, but because its context is "before God" it also knows a stripping of another sort: "My heart and flesh sing for joy to the living God"; "Let the word of Christ dwell in you richly, as you teach and admonish one another in all wisdom, and as you sing psalms and hymns and spiritual songs with thankfulness in your hearts to God"; or again, as Paul wrote to the Christian community at Corinth: "Open your hearts to us. . . . I do not say this to condemn you, for I said before that you are in our hearts to die together and to live together. I have great confidence in you; I have great pride in you; I am filled with comfort. With all our affliction, I am overjoyed." In how many of today's "moral" movies is there the remotest hint of what stripping *can* be?

I seriously would suggest that the only people who find true moral edification in films like *Woolf* are those

who, like the theologian-critics, have such a supply of
sophistication and Christian knowledge that they can disregard the exhibitionism and write into the script the "before God" context of which the film itself displays nothing.

What happens, you see, is that we turn an important
relationship head-end-to. Nudity and redemption do belong together, but not as though nudity were redemption
or stripping a way of getting ourselves redeemed. We
cannot become innocent simply by acting so, cannot get
back to Eden by going nudist. The fact is that we are
not free and cannot become so simply by acting freely. It
may be that any stripping—even the exhibitionism that
takes place in the godless context east of Eden—affords
a certain temporary catharsis. But it is a sad thing if this is
all we intend by "Christian morality."

No, the freedom to strip, to enjoy godly nudity, is a
gift that comes with redemption, not a method for attaining it. Therefore the proper context for Christian stripping and the only sort of stripping that deserves the ad-
jective "Christian" is that which is done before God, which
consciously is oriented toward him, which has been enabled by him, and which is dedicated to him as an act
of worship. It is in the Christian community that this
best can take place, in the redemptive fellowship where,
with our brethren before God (*before* God but *with* our
brethren, not *before* them), we can be bold to undress and
in so doing have our nudity hallowed.

King David stripped to the *soul* when, condemned by
the Lord through Nathan, he lay on the ground for seven
days. He stripped to the *skin* when he danced in ecstasy
before the Ark of the Lord. But if I may say so, what
Liz Taylor did in *Woolf* and what she promises to do in
Reflections in a Golden Eye are scenes from another picture.

Now for comment in more detail on *Who's Afraid of
Virginia Woolf?*—the one among the films listed by Boyd

which I have attempted to study seriously by referring to the playwright's own script. Not only is the "before God" aspect completely foreign to the play, but the evidence is that playwright Edward Albee's understanding of existence is such that the very concepts of "honesty," "reality," "truth," and "morality" go limp and slippery.

In the first place, I take it as obvious that *Woolf* is intended as a portrayal not simply of four individuals but of mankind in general and in essence. But the striking thing about Albee's human race is that every member of it (not only the four principals that appear but also, offstage, Honey's and Martha's fathers) is a fake, a living lie whose outward respectability clothes self-aggrandizement, greed, rapacity, callousness, indecency—you name it. It would be hard to point to an event, gesture, word, or deed in the play that represents anything remotely reminiscent of *agapē,* the only quality that the New Testament recognizes as "love." Let the admirers of *Woolf* herewith cease and desist from criticizing neo-orthodoxy's view of man; behold, rather, a picture of depravity that would make John Calvin throw in the towel—out of admiration if not out of disgust.

Albee's is a rather rough judgment on the human race. But thus far we have not established that his play is any more immoral than are Calvin's *Institutes.* It all depends upon what is taken to be the significance of and the solution for mankind's sham. Calvin saw it as signifying man's disorientation from God and as being solved when God, in his grace, steps in to rectify the relationship. We would not expect a secular playwright to come to precisely this answer, and Albee does not disappoint us. But Albee's is no answer at all.

One thing Albee does very effectively (and nothing I say is intended to detract from his eminent skill and power as a playwright) is to dissolve the distinction between illusion and reality. What is first presented as fact (maybe)—Nick's story of his marriage—is later presented as fiction—George's second novel. What was originally presented as fiction (maybe)—George's account of a boy he knew—becomes his first novel, which becomes his autobiography. Martha's fiction of her son becomes George's fiction of their son killed in the same way he had killed his father (if he had in fact killed his father).

The evening fun-time, which had started out with the game of Strip to the Buff (i.e., get to the truth about ourselves), winds up next morning with the game of Peel the Label (but a label is not a façade to hide the contents but precisely an identification of those contents). George is determined, he says, to go through the skin and through the muscle, slosh aside the organs, get to the bone, and then pierce it to the marrow. But by what definition is marrow more real than skin? By what standard is it so obvious that what people say to each other in *Woolf* is that much more honest than what they say to each other in church? Strip, strip, strip, strip! But without God and God-defined love, who is to decide when one has reached the "honest" level or gone clean past it into anarchy and nihilism? To rip away the truth of human existence is just as dishonest as to fail to rip away the sham.

Morning brings also the game of Snap Went the Dragons. Snap go the illusions! Yes. But when the distinction between truth and illusion is gone, snap go the truths as well; snap goes every string that had held the whole ball of wax together. Heads off all around—including mine! Nick complains, "I don't know when you people are lying, or what." Martha pleads, "Truth and illusion, George; you don't know the difference"; to which George retorts, "No, but we must carry on as though we did." Whereupon Martha intones "Amen." Again, Martha: "Truth or illusion, George. Doesn't it matter to you . . . at all?" "SNAP! [*Silence.*] You got your answer, baby?"

I would have to be convinced from the script that anything else is Albee's last word. The night of honesty arrives with the finding that all is sham. But to expose

everything as false is not to arrive at the truth—and far
less at the Truth of which the John Gospel has Jesus
speak, the Truth which shall make you free. Jesus too
knew about the game of Peel the Label, the ultimate sin
that loses the distinction between honesty and deception,
reality and illusion. I am not accusing Albee of the unforgivable sin; I am saying that his play accuses the universe of having committed that unforgivable sin against
mankind. *Woolf*'s search for honesty comes out at the
same cynical non-question that put Jesus on the cross:
"What is the truth—if there is such a thing?"

Yes, the language of *Woolf* is immoral and filthy—the
play's characters call it so themselves—but this is a minor
consideration in relation to the morality of the play itself.
What the play's characters do to one another is immoral,
even if they were to have done it in the language of little
ladies and gentlemen. It is immoral to lash another person
with hate, vituperation, and vindictiveness, to seek to humili-
ate him by making him look at himself in the worst possible
light—even if it is a true light.

But this immorality too is somewhat beside the point
until we find out what the author does with it, where it
leads. Yet, when the denouement of the play suggests that
the universe itself, the very nature of human existence, is
immoral—i.e., opaque to the distinction between good and
evil, truth and falsehood, reality and illusion—then there
can be no hint of redemption because, indeed, there is no
place from which redemption could come. Thus the play
is immoral in the most solemn and serious sense of that
word. And its message is that not only Martha but everyone would do well to be afraid of life, of Virginia Woolf.

True, some critics and viewers have found implications
of Christian morality in *Woolf*. But I contend that in so
doing they have read into the play presuppositions and in-
terpretations which cannot be supported by the text. That
they have found moral edification does not mean that Albee
deserves credit for having written a moral play. The Viet-

nam war, too, has aroused deep moral reflections in the minds of men who bring to it their own sense of Christian morality, but the war does not thereby become moral.

This "nude morality" article brought an interesting sequel. A Jewish rabbi, Gerald Lee Zelizer of Union, New Jersey, read the piece and picked up its major thrust as the basis of an article of his own which was published in the Jewish biweekly *Reconstructionist*.

(I don't know how much of the ethic of promise can be made applicable to Jewish thought. Of course, the basic concept of history and human existence on which it is based —i.e., history as a sequence that is end state oriented under the lordship of the God who is working to bring all things under his kingly rule—comes right out of the Old Testament. On the other hand, the assertion that Jesus Christ is the one through whom God makes the kingdom a possibility and even a present reality is bound to create problems for the Jewish brethren. But we claim no monopoly; they are welcome to as much of this eschatological ethic as they choose to buy.)

In any case, Rabbi Zelizer's article gave me an opportunity to enjoy a little interfaith dialogue and carry my thinking about the nude morality a little further at the same time. What follows is my letter which later appeared in *Reconstructionist*.

TO THE EDITOR:

Thank you for sending me a copy of the article by Gerald Lee Zelizer ("Have the Performing Arts Gone Too Far?" December 20, 1968) which borrows some of my ideas. Allow me to respond and keep this Christian-Jewish dialogue going for a little. Except for the spelling of my name (it is Eller, not Ellen) I am in full accord with the use to which Rabbi Zelizer puts my thinking, but I would like to carry *his* thinking just a step further.

He proposes that, in the context of stage and film presentations, nudity is proper if it denotes redemption or, as he has it, liberation. It would seem to follow that such edification would almost have to apply to the stripper (the one who undresses) rather than the beholder; it must be radically unself-conscious nudity—the very opposite of an *exhibitionism* that undresses precisely in order to be seen. With nudity in the performing arts, then, it must be the case that the playgoer identifies with the stripper to the point that his interest is not in seeing the bare actor but in empathetically stripping with him.

Once exhibitionism and the enjoyment of exhibitionism is thus outlawed, the problem becomes much more sticky even than trying to determine the intention of the playwright (the norm that Rabbi Zelizer sets up). The effect on the audience is the ultimate criterion. This brings other factors into our ethical problem; the advertising and reviews must be considered. Advertisers and reviewers know their public; and if they play up the fact that the show includes nudity (and how much performed nudity is there that does not get so played up?), this is an almost certain indicator of the exhibitionism the mass of playgoers will expect and are invited to find. The intentions of the playwright (although I have yet to be convinced that they always are as pure as protested to be) are little to the point if the publicity and the expectations of the audience are of a different sort.

All this is to say that our discussion has established only the theoretical possibility of a performed nudity that could be moral and edifying. To me it is very much an open question whether that has been achieved, or whether—in a culture that is as deeply exhibitionistic (read "conspicuous consumption" or just plain "show-off") as ours—it even is capable of achievement.

VERNARD ELLER

As we try now to get specific, our basic contention is that modern society faces a crisis regarding sex because it insists on making either too much or too little of it and can't seem to hit the balance that gets sex into its proper and healthy context. Again it is a case that "contextualism" proves to be as much the new morality's downfall as its strength.

The crazy aspect of the case is that both the underevaluation and the overevaluation of sex come out of one and the same sector of society, are promoted through the same group of magazines, books, and movies, as expressions of the same philosophy of life. The two views stand side by side and all mixed up together. Today's popular understanding of sex is very confused and ambiguous indeed. Let us see whether the ethic of promise can be of help in achieving a degree of clarity.

On the one hand, sex is puffed as a morally neutral activity, a bodily function designed to afford keen pleasure and a gratifying play of the senses. Thus it should be exercised naturally and uninhibitedly for what it is—the means of happy fun. If God made the palate so that it enjoys fine food, if he made the skin so that it enjoys the invigoration of a shower, and if he made the genitals so that they enjoy orgasm, then the obvious purpose of these organs is enjoyment, and it is contrary to nature to repress these drives. In fact, *immorality* is the move to repress; *morality* is the move that frees these inborn, God-given desires to find their inherent goal and satisfaction.

Out of this side of the mouth, sex is casual, as casual as eating and drinking—as casual as *Playboy* magazine's efforts to present its playmates as good-natured, fun-loving neighbor girls who are ever available for the innocent pleasures of a roll in the grass. Sex, indeed, is so casual and innocent and so uncomplicated that it does not even rate consideration as a moral issue affecting the destiny of man.

But out of the other side of the mouth, the sex act becomes the highest reach of the human spirit, the means by which one discovers and achieves his true humanity.

The kid is fighting an identity crisis, confused, unsure of

himself, doubtful of his own manhood; a deeply understanding woman gives him tea, sympathy, and sex—and
the boy is saved. Poor Rachel, came out of an impossible
home situation that had stifled her spirit, made her ingrown
and negative; a generous passer-by lays her—and behold,
resurrection!

In the modern repertoire is a good deal of song and poetry
(hymn and liturgy?) that steals the mood and language of
religion to describe the sex act. Sex says: "These things I
have given you, that my joy may be in you, and that your
joy may be full." "I have come that they may have life,
and have it abundantly." "Beloved, let us love one another;
for love is of God, and he who loves is born of God and
knows God. . . . He who has me has life; he who has not
me has not life." "So if I make you free, you will be free
indeed." (If this be blasphemy, it is not mine; it is that of
the age.) Sex now has become so high and holy that to be
sexual is what it means to be moral; sex is as moral as
prayer, a communion of even greater satisfaction, relevance,
and meaning.

Either of these assessments makes at least some sort of
sense by itself—if the other is kept strictly out of view. But
as soon as there is any sort of dalliance between them,
things start to get weird; the resultant doctrine is nothing
but misanthropy, a misanthropology. Take it that sex *is*
simply a natural bodily pleasure, the end of which is sensual
gratification. This is to say that it is basically an animal act
to be exercised largely as animals exercise it, as a giving of
free rein to one's impulses and instincts. Human sex is
simply a somewhat more sophisticated (and thus even more
enjoyable) version of animal sex.

Well and good! Whatever else man may be, there is no
denying that he also is an animal; and it is possible that
his sex life—as his eating, drinking, breathing, and elimination—is to proceed in a manner not radically different
from that of his fellow animals. But then to turn around
and suggest that *this* sex represents the highest experience

of which man is capable, that it marks the fulfillment of his personhood—this is to imply that man is nothing more than an animal (or at least that this particular animal function ranks above his superanimal functions). And it makes man a very low order of animal at that. Dogs have a higher calling; their destiny is to be "man's best friend," not merely to have ecstatic copulation. Society really ought to decide which way it wants it on sex; the two together add up to a major case of self-insult.

Of course, there is an advantage to having it both ways at once. When theologians attack *Playboy* magazine for demeaning sex, making it a mere plaything, one can point to serious articles and stories celebrating it as holy communion. When the movies are accused of making sex a god, one can point to other films (or even other places in the same film) where it is treated with a free and easy casualness. But playing upon contradictories is not the same thing as finding a balance.

Let's see if the ethic of promise can do better. For a starter, let it be admitted that the sex act is a natural bodily function which man shares with the rest of the animals and that it is one which normally is very enjoyable—real fun. As such sex *is* amoral, morally neutral; sex per se is neither good or bad—it just is. However, there is a difference that must be noted: When animals do it, it is animals that do it; when people do it, it is persons who do it. If we may put it so, genitals come attached to persons, and they cannot be operated independently of the persons to whom they are attached. Sex is morally neutral, but whatever affects the humanity of persons is precisely what we have defined as being morality. The question, then, has not to do with whether sex is moral or immoral but with what happens to persons as a consequence of their sexual activity.

One alternative is for the person to try and keep his personhood out of it. Why he should want to do this, suspend his humanity for the sake of "freeing" himself to be less than human, is one question. Whether he successfully *can* suspend his humanity is another question. The ethic of promise certainly will deny that he should *want* to. God's commitment, the character of his original creation, the thrust of his work in history, and the magnetism of his purpose and goal—all are in the direction of man's becoming more human rather than less so. As to whether man is *able* to suspend his humanity, both the ethic of promise and a great deal of human experience again would have to answer in the negative. Enough of the promise of the kingdom is built into man's very nature that any attempt to go against this grain ultimately will lead to frustration and tragedy. Man simply is unable to make sex work in the casual, amoral way that the animals achieve; the race already is too far committed to being human; man's genitals already are too solidly wired into his humanity.

If, then, man's destiny is to be human, what role is his sex destined to play in the service of that humanity? This alternative, rather than the one that would lead man to evade his humanity, is the one that might show some promise. Sex can be human and humanizing, because it can be a vehicle for expressing love. Love we already have defined; it is what God does, actions which promote his kingly rule and move men toward his eschatological intention for them. Sex can help do this. But notice that this does not make sex sacred—no more sacred than a lot of other activities that can express love. It is love that is sacred; sex can be a handmaiden to love, yet any hallowedness it possesses is due not to the sex act itself but to the love that is present.

Sex *can* be a vehicle for expressing love—although obviously it can also be a vehicle for expressing other things: selfishness, boredom, lust, pride, hatred. Yet even when devoted to the service of love, sex in some ways is a rather poor vehicle. For one thing, the very fact that it is so enjoyable is a temptation to use it selfishly rather than dedicate it to the other. For another, the passion involved can be so intense as to cloud and confuse the careful thought and intelligent concern which always must be an aspect of true

love. If, as we have suggested, love is an activity that is
end state oriented, then it cannot be simply the following
of impulses but requires rational forethought and planning.
Sex sometimes can get in the way of that.

Still, again, the sex act is too brief and fleeting to be
the best expression of love. Those are better expressions
that involve a continuing commitment, that show a willingness to stick by the other and serve him when things are
rough as well as fun, when one must do some giving without also getting immediate satisfactions in return. Although
Hollywood will never get rich proclaiming the fact, the
washing of dirty diapers usually marks a truer expression
of love than did the orgasmic ecstasy which went before.

All this is to say that if sex is to be a vehicle for expressing love, a means by which people truly help to human-
ize one another, it needs support and shoring up from some
other vehicles. Perhaps it is because sex does lie close to
the animal level of activity that it is too weak and unstable
to be an adequate love vehicle on its own, in and of itself.
The proper and necessary human context of sex, then, is
the quality of long-term, depth commitment that we call
"marriage."

By "marriage," we here intend this sort of stable man-
woman love commitment and nothing else—not a legal ar-
rangement, not a wedding ceremony. Obviously there are
any number of couples who have legal recognition but who
are not "married" in our sense of the term. And because
their sexual relationship does not have the support of a
marriage commitment, it is as far from moral as that sex
which more obviously is "outside of marriage." It follows,
too, that there may be couples who are "married" in the
fullest sense yet without the accompaniments of legal recognition and wedding ceremonies. Even the rigid old legalism of the state recognizes this possibility. There may be
exceptional circumstances (but recall our earlier protestations about "exceptions") in which marriage is true although
a wedding is impossible or inappropriate. Yet in such cases,

IN the heART

we would say, the sex relationship is "within marriage." At
the same time, however, we would insist that such exceptions
are going to be very rare. We already have noted how—
particularly from the perspective of the ethic of promise—
even a person's most private acts reflect his social involvement and are actions of one who is a part of humanity and
thus, with his fellows, a candidate for the kingdom. Persons
who feel this are going to *want* to give public attestation of
their marriage commitment, recognize the stake that society
has in it, and welcome society's support in their venture.
And society, for the sake of the proper operation of the
community, has the right to ask that couples do make these
commitments public knowledge.

So, from no source other than the new morality's "only"
law of love, there follows the law that sex plays its humanizing function and is therefore moral only within the context of "marriage." This, we would contend, is a law that
is just as valid as the law of love itself— because it is simply
a particular expression of that law. But let us recall what
a "law" is. A law is a *description* of what (in this instance)
true lovers will *want* to do and in fact do do. The possibility
of exceptions is not prohibited yet certainly not invited or
encouraged.

Casual sex, sex without true *agapé* love, is animality.
Authentic man-woman love wants, seeks, and takes the
form of "marriage"; and as a vehicle of "marriage-love,"
sex can be truly humanizing, a servant of the kingdom of
God—and that, we might say, with its "fun component"
enhanced rather than diminished. Sex per se may afford animal pleasure; but within a truly human context the pleasures
of sex are heightened in proportion to the height God has
placed man above the animals.

15

The Lovin' End
(*for Real*)

———————◆———————

It really isn't quite fair to the great book-buying public to repeat in one book what one already has said in another; it's double indemnity or something like that. However, authors do it all the time; it's just that I am naïve enough to call attention to the fact.

In *His End Up* (Abingdon, 1969) I developed the distinction between "actual" and "real" and in passing suggested it as a distinction between the new morality and what didn't have a name at that time but what in this book has become the ethic of promise. The distinction may mark the crux of our whole discussion, the basic difference that eschatological perspective contributes to ethical thought. In some ways it sums up all we have been trying to say; so it is offered here as our conclusion.

The new morality—and any other moral system that focuses simply upon present decisions regarding the present situation—necessarily takes as its premise that the actual men it addresses are real men. What they *are* sets the limits of the moral demands that can be made of them. The moral capabilities that are seen as possible for present men is the "given" within which the morality must work. The moral system represents the attempt to find the conditions under which *these* men most effectively can operate and best get along with one another. No reality is envisioned except

what actually obtains at present or is possible under the
conditions of the present.

The ethic of promise, conversely, starts from the premise
that men of the actual present are very far from being real
men. Their reality lies not in what they are but in what,
through the kingly rule of God, they are becoming. The
Vernard Eller you see before you—with all his hang-
ups, breakdowns, cave-ins, blowouts, flop-overs, and run-
arounds—is not the real, true, genuine Vernard Eller (let
all the people say "Amen!"). Hopefully, he is on the way
to becoming Vernard Eller, and someday, with God's help
(though assuredly not otherwise), he will make it. The race
you see before you is not the real, true, genuine human
race but is on its way toward humanity. The world which
you see before you is not the real, true, genuine world; it
will be when it has become the kingdom of God.

Reality, then, resides not in the actuality of what chances
to obtain at the moment; reality resides in what God has
planned, what he created for, what he has promised, what
he is working toward, what he will not rest until he has
accomplished. Moral teaching and guidance, then, should be
reality-oriented. The aim of morality is not to make human
existence tolerable under the conditions of the present but
to help move it toward its destiny. Its aim is not to make
a man comfortable in regard to what he is but to challenge
him to become what he can be and what God is offering
to make of him.

Such an ethic of promise is not unrealistic; the fact that
God has promised it, already has worked and is working
to bring it to pass, makes this future the only true reality.
Such an ethic is not oblivious to the present but sees the
present in its true light as being a moment on the way
toward tomorrow's reality. To focus upon the future, to step
out on the promise, to point toward the end state, is not
to ignore the present but to get it into context. On the
other hand, to center solely upon the actuality of the present, ignoring whither it came and whither it goes, is to rob

it of its potentiality, its pregnancy, its reality. The only way
to be true to the present is to use it for what it is, a step
toward the future.

And so the ethic of promise is a heroic morality, one that
really stretches men, one that calls them to act beyond what
they consider to be their capabilities (beyond what actually
are their capabilities were it not that a God stands by who
is ready to make human impossibilities possible). Such an
ethic calls for daring and risk, for faith, hope, and the most
self-abandoning sort of love; but how else—how else shall
the promise of the kingdom come to realization?

16

The Grand Irrelevancy
of the Gospel

——◆◇◆——

A Revelation
That Should Have Been Genesis

I suppose I should make some attempt to conceal what has happened here, but because I would as soon be hung for a fool as a deceiver, I tell it like it is. Obviously the preceding chapter was written to be the coda and grand finale of the book. And that is precisely the way the manuscript was submitted to the publisher and even started upon the manufacturing process. But then, months after I had finished writing, I suddenly discovered what my book is all about.

The problem is that I have not yet mastered the art of writing books. They tend to get away from me and rush ahead writing themselves while I am plodding along somewhere behind. Don't get me wrong; I have nothing but appreciation for the leading of the Holy Spirit. But if he takes so long a lead and fails to provide a little push and enablement at the same time, it can make for a very sloppy book.

I really don't know where this chapter belongs. It certainly is not an appendix—nearer to being the heart (or at least the gizzard) of the book. Perhaps it should be Chapter One or Two; perhaps in sequence with Chapter Six. But in any case, where it is going to have to be now is *here*.

The germ of my thought was in the covering letter written to accompany the manuscript of the book. (The letter actually got written some time after the manuscript already had been received and acknowledged by Doubleday—another evidence of my problem.) But I there wrote:

> This book is designed specifically to infuriate every possible reader. From the outset, of course, the new moralists are bound to take umbrage. Then we come to pacifism —a delight to liberals but anathema to conservatives. But wait; before my pacifism is well launched I specifically reject the liberal rationale for it and insert a theological base that is anything but the current liberal one. And then, a few chapters later, I am trying to make moral issues out of drinking, profanity, and sex—this time pleasing the conservatives and maddening the liberals. For every copy of this book you sell, I am going to have one fewer friend.

I wrote that to be cute; now I see that it may be profound. What it all amounts to is that this book is "irrelevant"—the most damning judgment that can be made. Yet I intend the opinion seriously. Reinhold Niebuhr is correct that, given man's conditions of sin, talk about love perfectionism is *irrelevant*. When we live in a world structured and outfitted as a football field and populated by football players, counsels of defenselessness are *irrelevant*. Claude Evans speaks to the point; when more than 60 per cent of adult Methodists already are drinking, for the Methodist Church to promote total abstinence is somewhat *irrelevant*. When *Hair* is the nation's No. 1 musical, to get uptight about *Hair*-styled language is—shall we say?—*irrelevant*. So let *me* say it before the reviewers get a chance to: This book is *irrelevant*.

Now granted, I was not too much bothered over being irrelevant, but I was thinking about it. And then, some time after I had sent in my manuscript and the covering letter, *The Christian Century* asked me to review a book (which review I choose *not* to reprint here; I do have some will power). But in that book there is a sentence that would not go away. It reads, "A Christian is a follower of Jesus Christ, not Don Quixote." As it stands, of course, the statement is unimpeachable; however, the clear implication is that, whereas the don was impractical, unrealistic, irrelevant, Jesus was just the opposite. But the thesis won't stand. It is, of course, very easy to make distinctions between Quixote and Jesus; yet regarding the point in question it just might be that Jesus comes off worse than Quixote. The more I consider the matter, the more I want to talk about "the grand irrelevancy of Jesus."

His basic trouble was that everything he said and did took for granted a kingdom of God which was nowhere in sight (to worldly eyes—which raises the point to which we shall get in due course) and which then as now was not even a live option. But because of that basic irrelevancy, every aspect of his strategy and method proves equally irrelevant. Let us use the temptation story recounted by Matthew and Luke (and interpreted by Gerhard Gloege) as the starting point for some examples.

In refusing to change stones into bread, Jesus rejected the relevant practicality that lies at the heart of *secularism,* namely the insight that the way to capture people's attention, interest, and following is to entice them with "goods," the possessions and enjoyments they want and even need. Fine; but if Jesus decided to renounce secularism he should have had the sense to choose *asceticism* and promote a spirituality that gives one credit for *disdaining* possessions and enjoyments. But poor old Jesus managed to be totally irrelevant; he missed the advantages of either alternative and caught trouble from both. He got himself called a glutton and drunkard yet without the compensations of having lived it up. His regimen actually was very austere, yet he was not able to come off as a "holy man" in the fashion of

St. Anthony. Irrelevant is what he was, choosing a strategy that could lead only to his getting himself killed.

Jesus' refusal to cast himself from the pinnacle of *the temple* can be interpreted as a rejection of the way of *ecclesiastical* advancement. Later, when Nicodemus came by night, it was a once in a lifetime opportunity for making it with the Sanhedrin; but Jesus threw away his big chance. OK, if he doesn't choose to use the temple to his own advantage, he should have sense enough to catch the advantage of destroying it; he would have made a fine iconoclast. But what does his iconoclasm come to? A one-man, flash-in-the-pan demonstration in the temple that didn't change a thing and served only to get himself killed. And right in the middle of a beautiful assault on ecclesiasticism ("You have heard that it was said, . . . but I say to you") he manages to drop the line: "Think not that I have come to abolish the law . . . not an iota will pass away." What under the sun does the man have in mind? Irrelevant is what he is, and dead is how he will wind up.

Jesus' refusal to accept the kingdoms of the world can be taken as a rejection of the power of the *political* establishment. Well, that makes sense—if he has intentions of replacing that establishment with one of his own. But why, then, did he scorn the zealots? Comes the confrontation, the moment of truth, catch the command to his troops: "Put your sword back into its place; for all who take the sword will perish by the sword!" Is one supposed to laugh or to cry? And then, when it is all over, what could be more pathetic: "If my kingship were of this world, my servants would fight [but since it is not, I guess the best we can do is to die]"? When, obviously, it is the kingdoms of the world that determine the way it is, an appeal to some absent, invisible, powerless kingdom of God is about as absolute an irrelevancy as can be conceived.

The way we have described it, one might assume that Jesus' strategy was the attempt to hit the golden mean, that he saw himself as the reconciler who, from his place in the center, builds bridges toward the extremes on either side. Now that is a nice strategy, to be sure, but there is no evidence that it was Jesus'. If so, he certainly made a botch of it, for he managed to offend everyone involved; successful bridge builders usually don't get crucified for it. Rather, Jesus' strategy (if he had one) appears as a wobbly zigzagging that is oblivious to all the relevant alignments and structures of the world—and furthermore, a wobbling that reaped no advantage from any of the territories traversed yet gained the enmity of all. He couldn't have been more irrelevant if that is what he had set out to be.

If relevancy is to be our norm, Christians might do well to follow Don Quixote instead of Jesus. Jesus was grandly irrelevant—and his end on the cross proves it. A cross— the completely ineffectual powerlessness of the cross, with evil in the driver's seat and the disciples scattered in betrayal, denial, and despair—this is the true end of the irrelevant way of Jesus. It should be clear that the resurrection is *not* the end of the way of Jesus—and the New Testament nowhere suggests that it was. The way of Jesus did not create, did not lead to, is not continuous with the resurrection; that was a eucatastrophe, an overturning, an intervention that canceled out the consequences of Jesus' way, not that was one of them. No note of the gospel is plainer than that of the sheer irrelevancy of Jesus.

We have said it, and although it be in defiance of the most popular dictum of modern Christian thought, we intend it with all seriousness: The way of Jesus was one grand irrelevancy. Yet obviously the matter is not to be left at this point. Rather, the discussion should lead to a very careful consideration of what it means to be "relevant." An action is relevant when it makes sense *from the perspective that obtains*. This conditional phrase suggests, then, that there are two different ways of being irrelevant: Either the action simply does not make sense—*or,* it is not being viewed from the perspective in which it would make sense.

Ponder that last for a moment. You probably have seen

the sort of puzzle in which a message is inscribed in extremely elongated print; with very thin verticals and very fat horizontals, the letters are stretched into veritable illegibility. However, once the message is viewed from a very low angle, it becomes easily readable. From the perspective of the perpendicular, then, normal type is relevant and the elongations of the puzzle irrelevant; but switch to the perspective of the horizontal and the relevancy is exactly reversed. I happened upon an even more impressive example recently. An article included a description and photograph of an oil painting done in the eighteenth century. Viewed normally, the painting consists of irrelevant swirls and swatches. However, if the painting is laid flat and a chrome-plated cylinder stood upon it at the proper spot, the reflection of the painting caught upon the sides of the cylinder forms a perfect picture. Relevancy and irrelevancy are entirely dependent upon perspective.

What we just did, then, was to view the way of Jesus from the perspective of the world, its evaluations and modes of thought. But switch once to Jesus' own perspective, that of the oncoming kingdom of God, and the picture is entirely different. Now, rather than wobbling, Jesus' way is seen to be pointed straight for the kingdom. It is the worldly structures and alignments that now are seen to be crazily askew. Wobble there is indeed, but it is not Jesus'.

Here, then, is the explanation for our earlier insistence that the same ethic cannot do for both the church and the world, that the church has a secret discipline of its own which is different from its counsel to the world. If the New Testament makes anything clear it is that the gospel operates out of a perspective different enough from that of the world that inevitably one will be somewhat irrelevant to the other. Let us beware, then, of the popular cry that the church must become relevant. Once "relevant" (in this sense) and it is no longer the church; it has forsaken its unique perspective to become simply a part (even if, perhaps, a "better" part) of the world.

In the course of our book we have developed the differences between the two perspectives—although we may not have been entirely conscious of what we were doing. The perspective of the world is that of "the actual," the here and now, the conditions that pertain at this place, at this time, and to humanity as it presently exists. Relevant actions, accordingly, are those that can be calculated to ameliorate those conditions, that can be seen as capable of changing the present situation into another which is directly continuous with it. Present conditions and present possibilities are determinative. And from this standpoint, actions premised upon a future which is not yet apparent, pointing toward options which are not yet possible—these are bound to seem irrelevant.

The perspective of the gospel, on the other hand, is that of "the real." And the reality toward which it looks is that of the future—specifically, God's future, that of his intention, will, and purpose, that of his promise, commitment, and covenant. Being *God's* future, it is to be expected that it lies beyond man's control, beyond man's manipulations (however well intended), beyond man's utopian constructs, beyond what man can envision even as possibility. The relevant, now, is that which is done in obedience to this God of the future—even if man's limited capability and foresight mean that at times his must be *blind* obedience (obedience that leads to a cross which would seem to spell the end of everything). And from this perspective, much of what here and now is considered so weighty and significant becomes strangely irrelevant.

So, we maintain, the irrelevancy of the Christian ethic, rather than being something to be regretted, adjusted, or overcome, is the very sign of its glory. Yet, obviously, we do not mean to glorify irrelevancy in and of itself; only that which ignores worldly regiment in order to be relevant to the kingdom deserves commendation. But it must be confessed that many Christians and churches manage to be irrelevant both to the world and to the kingdom. They are found to be relevant only from the perspective of some dead past or from no perspective at all. What, then, will be the style and look of true Christian irrelevancy?

Our cue comes from the "political theology" of Johannes B. Metz, Roman Catholicism's leading theologian of hope. His term is bound to be grossly misleading, but he is with us—talking of the "politics" of God, of citizenship in the city of God which is the kingdom—rather than with the social-action contextualists who seem to know nothing but the politics of this world. He describes the Christian stance as demonstrating *liberty* from the world and as being *critical* of the world.

Because the church's perspective is radically different from that of any worldly party, so must its actions be. Thus, although at points these actions may coincide with those of some worldly agency, the church dare never allow herself to become captured by, aligned with, "unequally yoked" (as Paul has it) to any party, ideology, or movement. The church at all times must be free to follow its own call, march to its own Drummer. This means, certainly, that Christian irrelevancy dare not be equated with the irrelevancy of liberalism to conservatism or of conservatism to liberalism. If a church finds itself regularly siding with secular liberalism against the conservatives, or with secular conservatism against the liberals, it had better look to itself to see whether it has not exchanged its kingdom birthright for a mess of this world's pottage. The Christian's way through the world should bear some resemblance to that of Jesus. It should be the zigzag that defies political categorization, that cuts across worldly alignments rather than following them. It should be the zigzag that, from the gospel perspective, is seen to be the straight thrust that shows up the party lines of the world for the wobbly scrawls they are.

When the church fails to guard this liberty, she gets sucked into a pseudoeschatology that mistakes "the world of tomorrow" for the oncoming kingdom. Now, although the church merely shares the world's perspective, the assumption gets made that the gospel somehow imparts to Christians a political expertise and wisdom, a political integrity and piety, that is superior to that of other men. The church takes on the role of doting mother to the world, the sort of woman who loves her little boy so much that she wheedles, cajoles, bribes, badgers, nags, and "loves" him into being what she wants him to be. "Mamma knows best!" And today the church seems very quick to tell the world how to get itself straightened out—even though the church is having manifest troubles in getting herself straightened out. Perhaps that is precisely the psychology involved, that of the person who hides from his own problems by becoming counselor to others.

Yes, the church does have a claim to the wisdom of her unique perspective. She has the right and indeed the obligation to proclaim that wisdom and seek to win men to that perspective. But this is far from being the same thing as claiming the worldly wisdom to tell the world how to run its business and live out the implications of its perspective. Just because one has received the grace of learning basketball, it does not follow that he can tell football players how to play their game. It is precisely this attitude of worldly superiority, I am convinced, that has led to much of the world's resentment against the church—and the laity's resentment against the clergy.

Consider too that this role does not spell freedom from the world any more than the doting mother is free from her little boy. Although fancying herself as superior to, she actually is completely tied to and dependent upon him, because her entire worth and fulfillment depend upon how well he responds to her manipulations. In the same way, the modern church tends to measure its worth by how much it can accomplish in changing the world into what the church thinks it ought to be.

True liberty, it must be said, is not all that concerned

with the repercussions of its own actions—just as Jesus does not seem to have spent a lot of time checking out the social consequences of his activity, as to whether or not he was making progress in getting the world reformed. James suggests that a double-minded man, unstable in all his ways, cannot expect anything from the Lord. And it is a double-mindedness to want to be fully obedient to God on the one hand and to have to gauge one's accomplishments in the world on the other.

I have become more and more impressed with Jesus' statement: "No one who puts his hand to the plow and looks back is fit for the kingdom of God." The church truly is free only when it plows straight for the kingdom— let the clods fall where they may. Of course, Christian obedience does bring consequences; but these—if we may put it so—are God's worry. Of course, Christian obedience has touched off revolutions and turned the world upside down—both the New Testament and Christian history testify to the fact. Yet this is not to say that Christians are revolutionaries concerned to plot and engineer social change. Quite the contrary, they plow blithely toward the kingdom while the world is turned over behind them, as it were. But how it turns or even whether it turns is not their business. If there is any significance in calling it "the kingdom *of God*," it is that he is capable of handling the how and the whether. That Christians have a liberty in respect to the world means that it is not our responsibility to make it come out right; let us take care of our obedience, and let God take care of the world.

Yet of course, the Christian happens also to be a citizen; and, as a citizen, he has some specific allegiances and responsibilities to the world of which he is a part. But the suggestion that his being a Christian changes the character of his citizenly responsibility is a questionable thesis indeed—particularly if it be implied that he thus acquires special authority and status. Because the structure of society, its playing field, is laid out according to the perspective of the world rather than that of the gospel, from a Christian point of view the political options available under such a setup necessarily are going to be limited and ambiguous. Worldly alignments do not readily provide Christian alternatives. In most if not all political choices there is likely to be some of truth and some of falsehood on either side, on all sides. There is no Christian party, no Christian position, no Christian possibility; from the start, the situation has been ordered from the wrong perspective.

Nevertheless, as citizen, the Christian is going to have to pick his way through these mazes—just as the non-Christian citizen is going to have to. Perhaps the church can be of assistance in helping the citizen think the matter through, but both the church and the Christian had better be very cautious about making dogmatic proclamations as to which is *the* Christian position, as to where all true Christians must or must not stand. (And let it be noted that, on their pet issues, the conservative churches are just as guilty in this regard as the liberal churches are on theirs.) The church is to exercise liberty, and "taking sides" (in the sense of becoming identified with one party or another) is an erosion of that liberty. The church's primary responsibility is to be true to her own perspective —even at the cost of seeming irrelevant.

The second hallmark of the church, Metz suggests, is that it be *critical* of the world. This, I am suggesting, is not to say that the church has been given a divine appointment as faultfinder to the world, that its job is to berate and complain. Rather, in its freedom, by being what it is called to be, the very presence of the church stands as a critique of the world. The church does not have to sponsor a program of world criticism; when the church is itself the critical function is cared for automatically. As always, Jesus is the paradigm: "If anyone hears my sayings and does not keep them, I do not judge him; for I did not come to judge the world but to save the world. He who rejects me and does not receive my sayings has a judge; the word that I have spoken will be his judge on the last day" (John 12:47–48). Although Jesus was hardly what one could call "judgmental," his life (and particularly his death at the hands of the world) constitutes the most radical judgment of the world that has been made. With complete consistency the Gospel author can in one chapter have Jesus say, "I judge no one" (John 8:15), and in the very next chapter have him say, "For judgment I came into this world" (9:39). Surely, the church's critique of the world is to be of the same order.

Quite clearly, one outstanding feature of the world (and inevitably so, given its perspective that the truth of things is to be found in the actuality of the moment) is its *frenzy*. Today more than ever it is apparent that we live in a frenzied world. Liberals are in a frenzy to eliminate war, poverty, and racism *now*—no matter how much ill will, backlash, militancy, and destruction are created in the process. Conservatives are just as frantic to "save" law and order, public morality, the American way of life. And the demand that the church must become "relevant" is nothing but a prod toward joining the stampede.

But the perspective of the gospel should point toward a somewhat different conclusion. Its conviction that "God is the ruler yet" militates against impatience and panic restiveness. The word of the gospel is "Cool it," or, putting lines from Browning's "Rabbi ben Ezra" into a cosmo-historical rather than his individualized context:

> Grow old along with me!
> The best is yet to be,
> The last of life, for which the first was made:
> Our times are in His hand
> Who saith "A whole I planned,
> Youth shows but half; trust God: see all nor be afraid!"

So let the Christian live free of frenzy and in that life be formed as a critique and judgment upon the frenzy of the world. Patient in her deliberate irrelevance and seeming ineffectiveness, let the church resist the demand for "results," the temptation to grasp for whatever kingdom can be cobbled together in the moment. For what tragedy it would be to choose "relevance," go for quick "results," and miss the slower but infinitely greater "kingdom which God has promised to those who love him."

In the final analysis, then, for the church to exercise *liberty* from the world and to mount a *critique* of the world come to the same thing, namely to plow straight toward the kingdom without regard for the world. "Without regard for the world"—what a true description of the style of Jesus and the call of the church, and yet how utterly false! For, of course, the way of Jesus and his church exists solely *for the sake of that world;* and Christians are to do their disregarding right out in the midst of that world where it is sure to be noted. Just as the frontier doctor, amputating without the aid of anesthetics, had to disregard the cries, protests, curses, and struggles of the patient *for the sake of the patient,* just so does the Christian disregard the world. This is the grand irrelevancy of the gospel. To the death (literally to the martyrdom of the cross) will the Christian defend his right to be irrelevant, for only by being irrelevant to the actuality of the moment which the world understands as its truth can he be relevant to the reality of the oncoming kingdom which Christianity understands as the very truth of God, man, and the world.